LIBRARY
NEXT

ALA Editions purchases fund advocacy, awareness, and accreditation programs for library professionals worldwide.

LIBRARY NEXT

SEVEN ACTION STEPS *for* REINVENTION

CATHERINE MURRAY-RUST

CHICAGO 2021

Catherine Murray-Rust retired in August 2020 as the dean of libraries at the Georgia Institute of Technology. For more than forty years she has been a change agent, reimagining library services and collections to meet the needs of the community. Now she focuses on telling encouraging stories and offering practical advice about how to help libraries thrive in the future.

© 2021 by Catherine Murray-Rust

Extensive effort has gone into ensuring the reliability of the information in this book; however, the publisher makes no warranty, express or implied, with respect to the material contained herein.

ISBN: 978-0-8389-4839-2 (paper)

Library of Congress Cataloging-in-Publication Data
Names: Murray-Rust, Catherine, 1948- author.
Title: Library Next : seven action steps for reinvention / Catherine Murray-Rust.
Description: Chicago : ALA Editions, 2021. | Includes bibliographical references and index. | Summary: "This book shares the story of one library's attempt to stand up for the core values that all libraries share while fundamentally changing the way it achieves those values. It offers encouragement and practical advice for libraries and librarians on how to strengthen their skills and make a positive impact on the communities they serve"—Provided by publisher.
Identifiers: LCCN 2020045658 | ISBN 9780838948392 (paperback)
Subjects: LCSH: Academic libraries—Planning—United States—Case studies. | Academic libraries—Professional relationships—United States—Case studies. | Organizational change—United States. | Murray-Rust, Catherine, 1948- | Georgia Institute of Technology. Library and Information Center—Reorganization.
Classification: LCC Z675.U5 M874 2021 | DDC 027.70973—dc23
LC record available at https://lccn.loc.gov/2020045658

Cover photographs © David Hamilton. Book composition in the Skolar Latin and Gotham typefaces.

♾ This paper meets the requirements of ANSI/NISO Z39.48-1992 (Permanence of Paper).

Printed in the United States of America
25 24 23 22 21   5 4 3 2 1

Contents

vii / Preface

ix / Acknowledgments

1 Why Turn Yourself and Your Library toward Your Community?   1

2 Begin with Yourself   9

3 **Action Step One:** Look Outside Your Social Circle, Profession, and Organization for Ideas and Inspiration   17

4 **Action Step Two:** Be Curious about the Future   27

5 **Action Step Three:** Make Bold, Public Plans   39

6 **Action Step Four:** Cultivate Relationships with Allies and Champions   49

7 **Action Step Five:** Create Successful Change   63

8 **Action Step Six:** Implement a Framework for Action and Innovation   73

9 **Action Step Seven:** Focus on Impact   83

93 / Conclusion: Onward!

95 / Appendix A   Georgia Tech Library Revised Mission, Vision, Values, and Expected Behaviors

99 / Appendix B   Georgia Tech Library Portfolio Management Example: Price Gilbert Computing Technology Project Status Report

101 / Index

Preface

> Writing a book, just like building a library, is an act of defiance. It is a declaration that you believe in the persistence of memory.
> —Susan Orlean, *The Library Book*

While I was writing this book, COVID-19 turned our world upside down. At the time, I was at my daughter's home in Virginia helping take care of her newborn daughter and trying to keep up with news from Georgia Tech and libraries around the country. I stayed home as the e-mails flowed in from colleagues who were all struggling to do the right thing for their employees, colleagues, and communities. When I learned about how long the virus survives on plastic and cardboard, and the recommendations for all of us to keep at least six feet apart and wear a mask, I could no longer insist that libraries are safe havens. For the first time in my career, I recommended closing all physical library locations indefinitely and not allowing borrowing.

Life during the pandemic is teaching us important lessons about community, equity, and inclusion. We all need to become better at planning for all kinds of futures, the ones we like and the ones we would rather not have to face. We all need to be in touch with every segment of our community, not just those with the most resources or the loudest voices. We all need to be continuously focused on fulfilling the aspirations of the individuals and groups we serve. We all need to constantly work to make our collections and services equitably available by securing infrastructure and financial support for our communities as well as our libraries. We all need to keep engaging others while growing ourselves.

For more than forty years, I have worked to ensure that our libraries and our profession thrive. I often challenge other library leaders about what they are doing to positively impact library services today and in the years ahead. Many sorrowfully tell me that their spaces are shrinking, and their budgets are stagnant. Like me, they reject the call to stop using the word library because it is too old-fashioned to garner funding and public support. Some bemoan how hard it is to deal with rapid change. Others want help in creating a positive future and they want it now.

In my presentations and writing, I plead for librarians to focus on delivering digital services at scale and viewing the library's online presence as its primary, not secondary, service. Now, with all the pandemic-imposed changes, I take no pleasure in being right. I have no wish to yell, "I told you so." I hate the fact that a virus has scared us all into paying attention. I wish we and our institutions were better prepared to deliver content and services efficiently and effectively online. I wish every household in the country had affordable internet access for learning as well as entertainment. I wish our websites were beautiful, functional portals to all the library has to offer to everyone in the community.

I am writing this book to help all of us who value libraries to face squarely and come to terms with our uncertain future. We all suspect that hoping for the best, while planning for the worst, will not work. Deep down, we know that our fate is in our own hands. Waiting patiently and quietly to be appreciated and funded is not likely in this hyper-competitive world. We are committed to offering information expertise, innovative services, high-quality content, and inspirational facilities, but we lack resources. We struggle to replace the stereotype of shushing librarians protecting their books with one of outgoing library employees engaged with their communities and actively promoting their patrons' aspirations. We fear we do not have the skills to achieve intense cultural change, attract outstanding employees and partners, and encourage the bold ideas required for success.

Based on the lessons I learned during my years as a self-described library disrupter, in this book I offer you action steps to navigate these rapidly changing times and prepare for a brighter future. I encourage you to explore, share, practice, apply, and evaluate strategies and solutions that are compatible with your leadership style and are effective in your organizational environment. By reading my library work-life stories, especially tales from the twelve years I spent on the transformation of the Georgia Tech Library, and by applying my recommended takeaways to your work, you will strengthen your leadership qualities and strategic skills—courage, integrity, empathy, collegiality, and kindness.

Acknowledgments

Writing this book has been a walk down memory lane for me. I am honored to know and remember the creative, courageous, and kind people with whom I have worked in my forty-plus years as a librarian. Many of you appear in these stories. Even though I cannot list everyone by name, I am grateful for you in my life.

I especially thank my Georgia Tech Library colleagues for twelve years of enthusiasm and hard work turning the library toward our community. You have made a positive impact on the lives of students and faculty by increasing the good the library does in the world. I wish you all the best as you keep learning, growing, and changing in the years ahead.

Thank you also to my colleagues at Emory University Libraries for your willingness to join with Georgia Tech to make our mutual dreams come true. The Library Service Center and the shared collection are a reality because of our partnership. You renewed my faith in the power of collaboration.

Thank you to the architects, designers, and construction experts at Georgia Tech, BNIM, and Praxis3 for welcoming us library folks as co-creators of beautiful, renovated spaces. To brightspot strategy for teaching us how to engage the community in making better decisions for the future. To Georgia Tech Strategic Consulting for helping us develop a framework for action while managing the joys and sorrows of major organizational change. To the Georgia Tech leadership and the University System of Georgia for supporting our vision politically and financially. Thank you all.

Georgia Tech Library 2014 and 2020, south side
Photograph by David Hamilton

Why Turn Yourself and Your Library toward Your Community?

> I am of the opinion that my life belongs to the whole community, and as long as I live it is my privilege to do for it what I can.
> —George Bernard Shaw, *Man and Superman*

IN PREPARATION FOR AN ANNUAL LEADERSHIP RETREAT, MY BOSS AT THE Georgia Institute of Technology asked another dean on campus and me to write a case study about the library's transformation, for discussion by a cohort of faculty members who were on a fast track to becoming deans and provosts. We carefully prepared our presentation and questions, but the retreat was canceled because of a campus tragedy two days before it was to take place. When we finally made our presentation several months later, the faculty engagement discussion was replaced by a short presentation plus a question-and-answer session. It did not go well.

At the time, many of the faculty participants were heavily involved in their own campus issues and had no time or interest to spare on the library's ambitious renovation project. Annoyance and irritation were everywhere in the room. When we got to question time, one engineering faculty member looked me in the eye defiantly and declared that he really did not see the point of spending all this time and money on the library when he never used it and didn't know anyone who did.

After pausing for a minute so I would not say something I would truly regret, I asked, "So, you don't use IEEE, Science Direct, Web of Science, or any of the other engineering publications?"

"Of course I do," he said, looking offended, "but I get them from Google."

1

"And how," I asked, "do you think they get to Google, since we pay millions on your behalf every year for subscriptions?"

"Oh," he said, looking a little less belligerent but not contrite. "You guys do that?"

This conversation did not surprise me. I had been having similar ones for years. It reminded me once again that as hard as my colleagues and I try to involve the campus community in the transformation of the library, we make little progress. We are grateful that there is minimal hostility to the changes we are making, but we're chagrined that the usual reaction is indifference. We constantly repeat our slogans about the library offering inspirational digital and physical spaces, curated scholarly content, information expertise, and outstanding services, but we have mixed results in engaging the campus.

I was slow to realize that we are making minimal progress getting people excited about our dreams for the future, because they are just that—our dreams for the future, not theirs. Our aspirations still are not deeply rooted in the community's aspirations. Our rhetoric is still too often about what we want for the community, not what the community wants for itself. Although we convinced the university to invest almost $120 million on the renovation of two campus library buildings and the construction of the Library Service Center (LSC) to house a shared collection with Emory University, we still have not captured the campus's imagination about the enhanced impact the library could have in the future. The library's long history of staying turned inward, relying on its own assessment of the needs of the community, and expecting users to come to it is hard to change. We have a long way to go before the library is a trusted, equal partner in helping the campus community achieve its aspirations.

If you are reading this, I assume you are curious about whether my stories and advice can help you and your library. You may work in a university or a city that invests heavily in its library. You may be part of a library that is a valued, integral part of the community. Your library buildings may be beautiful safe havens for people. You may have collections that meet the needs of children, seniors, and everyone in-between. If so, consider yourself fortunate; you have probably implemented several of the action steps in this book already. If not, I have some recommendations and suggestions for you.

But before we get to specifics, I strongly urge you and your colleagues to feel a sense of urgency about initiating change. The pandemic, racial injustice, violence, and all the other societal traumas we are experiencing have intensified the need for libraries at a time when our future is at risk. Some libraries are growing, and many are surviving, but few are thriving. When that fast-track faculty member or up-and-coming politician who never uses the library and doesn't know anyone who does becomes a university president or a mayor, we are usually in deep trouble. If we are lucky, they hear from community activists who will stand up for us. But without funding and political support, we will become increasingly marginalized and irrelevant. Failing to live up to the values we profess in the ALA Code of Ethics and the Library Bill of Rights will be obvious only to ourselves. Our communities will eventually abandon us in favor of individuals and organizations that deliver what they need.

To avoid this bleak future, we will have a better chance at a bright tomorrow if we turn our library from a "fortress" existing apart from the community to a "platform" for learning and discovery, both online and in person. You may be offended at my calling your library a "fortress." You may be wondering what "turning toward the community" really means. You may ask why it's not sufficient to do what we have always done, only better. You may disagree with my contention that libraries are vulnerable and need to change in order to thrive. But you don't have to take my word for it; look around you in this time of change and pay attention to the growing number of people who have the same view of libraries as my dismissive faculty colleague—although they may not be bold enough to tell you this to your face. We have to stop believing that we are intrinsically worthy and entitled to community support just because we believe we are. More humility and servant leadership would serve us well.

Libraries have been supported for the past 200 years in the United States by both public funding and private philanthropy. Enoch Pratt, Andrew Carnegie, Bill and Melinda Gates, and others invested heavily because libraries help individuals and communities grow and thrive. Whether these philanthropists' motivation was to provide for those less fortunate, strengthen the quality of the labor force, or promote civic harmony, they believed that libraries were a good investment. Among today's tech billionaires, Bill and Melinda Gates are among the very few who support libraries in any way. Our funding now comes primarily from public sources that are under severe pressure. We have to compete for support in ways we never had to before, and that means we need new ways of working to make a visible and sustainable impact on our communities.

In the past, libraries were masters of changing to meet community needs. Michael Gorman wrote a few years ago that libraries are the marriage of practicality and inspiration, and the history of libraries is the history of innovations to meet the needs of people, especially the ones most vulnerable in society.[1] In the nearly 200 years since the first tax-supported public library in the world opened in Peterborough, New Hampshire, libraries have provided reading material, quiet spaces, story times, literacy classes, small business development help, computer education, internet connections, and a host of other services to people in their communities.

Today, we have Professor Eric Klinenberg and the journalist Susan Orlean to thank for taking up the cause of libraries and making the case for their value. In her passionate book about the arson fire that nearly destroyed Los Angeles's Central Library in 1986, Orlean notes, "The publicness of the public library is an increasingly rare commodity. It becomes harder all the time to think of places that welcome everyone and don't charge any money for that warm embrace."[2]

In *Palaces for the People: How Social Infrastructure Can Help Fight Inequality, Polarization, and the Decline of Civic Life*, Klinenberg writes:

> Today, as cities and suburbs reinvent themselves, and as cynics claim that government has nothing good to contribute to that process, it's important that institutions like libraries get the recognition they deserve. After all, the root of the word "library," *liber*, means both "book" and "free." Libraries stand for and exemplify something that needs defending: the public institutions that—even in an age of atomization and inequality—serve as bedrocks of civil society. Libraries are the kinds of places where ordinary people with different backgrounds, passions, and interests can take part in a living democratic culture. They are the kinds of places where the public, private, and philanthropic sectors can work together to reach for something higher than the bottom line.[3]

I am grateful to these concerned supporters of libraries for making our case, but I am worried that we in libraries are not doing enough, quickly enough to change how we work together and relate to our communities. If we do not turn ourselves and our libraries toward our communities, we will not have the opportunity to make a difference in people's lives. That warm embrace that Susan Orlean writes about will no longer be free, if it still exists at all.

We need widespread, well-publicized efforts by those of us who work in libraries to confidently speak up about the value we add. Although every library is unique in its history, geography, and community, we all share the same mission, one that goes back centuries. We need to build on that shared mission to develop visions and strategies that are deeply embedded in the communities we serve. We need to change the way we work in order to become efficient providers of collections and services in tune with current and prospective users. We need to demonstrate the positive impact we have on the lives of individuals and groups.

In this book, I present stories and action steps based on my experience as a librarian for over forty years. These stories are about my colleagues and I standing up for the values we share with others in all kinds of libraries, while radically changing the way we achieve those values. You will accompany us as we work to transform the Georgia Tech Library from an inwardly focused provider of services and content to an outwardly facing community partner in learning and discovery. You will read about the joys and sorrows of a major building renovation that grew into the total transformation of the library and its relationship with the campus.

To make these ideas practical as well as inspirational, I start with a chapter about first beginning with yourself. By relating some deeply personal stories about my ongoing struggle to learn how to balance courage with kindness, I offer you several suggestions to explore that will help you become more creative and engaged with others.

Seven of the next eight chapters focus on action steps for you to consider. Each chapter features stories about my work life, mostly from the last twelve years at Georgia Tech. I offer you takeaways as well as suggested activities with which to explore, share, practice, apply, and evaluate your progress. A few chapters include an "imagine-you-are" story to illustrate how a fictional librarian went about implementing the action step for that chapter. Each action step is important to building libraries that can thrive today and tomorrow. All seven steps together constitute a strategy that I am offering you.

Action Step One: **Look outside your social circle, profession, and organization for ideas and inspiration**

The stories in this chapter are about all the ways my colleagues and I looked for inspiration outside our library. Because we were convinced that the most successful nonprofits and commercial organizations constantly try to learn from the experience of others, we set out to make new contacts. We already knew that the best ideas to help solve library problems, such as building environmentally sound, high-density storage facilities, are from other industries. Curiosity about how others tackle tough issues and make choices will help you deal with daily operational issues and anticipate major challenges ahead. In addition to urging you to travel and experience other workplaces, you will be introduced to information interviewing by a librarian named Jenny.

Action Step Two: **Be curious about the future**

The stories in this chapter focus on our efforts to engage others in anticipating the future at Georgia Tech and making better choices in the present. I include several methods of thinking about and planning for the future. You will read about scenario planning, working with a consulting firm to solicit community input and create a playbook, and participating in a Harwood Institute and American Library Association initiative. You will meet Pat, a fictional librarian who uses a simple four-part grid to consider options and decide how to move forward.

Action Step Three: **Make bold, public plans**

The story in this chapter is about developing and advocating for the Georgia Tech Library's 2020 plan, which eventually became the key to securing support and funding for the library's renovation. You will read about how we dramatically built our case and challenged the university to listen to us. You will learn how we sold our ideas to campus leadership. This chapter is a call to action, encouraging you to seek partnerships, not ask permission or wait for support.

Action Step Four: **Cultivate relationships with allies and champions**

The collaboration between Georgia Tech and Emory University to build the Library Service Center (LSC) and house a shared collection is the main story in this chapter. I also relate my experiences advocating for high-density storage facilities that would free up space in library buildings in three other institutions. You will read about the importance of allies and champions to help you succeed or encourage you to keep going when you fail. You will also meet an imaginary librarian named Yusef who is seeking allies and champions for his idea of hosting a digital art exhibit.

Action Step Five: Create successful change
Unlike the other stories, the main one in this chapter is a cautionary tale about my underestimating the power of organizational culture to resist change. It includes my insights into what I might have done differently to achieve more positive outcomes. I encourage you to proceed with your plans, but not introduce too many changes, too quickly. I remind you to make sure that the others on your team are on board, and to provide clear transitions from the present to the future. Again, in this chapter I base my recommendations on exploring, sharing, practicing, applying, and evaluating your progress.

Action Step Six: Implement a framework for action and innovation
This action step is about setting up a formal structure for designing and implementing your bold plans. You will read about my colleagues and I choosing "project portfolio management" to organize our work on the renovation of our library buildings and the transformation of library services, with the help of Georgia Tech Strategic Consulting (GTSC). As we did, I suggest you investigate the organizational techniques used in the technology industry, primarily for product development, in order to inform your choices. I make a plea for creating an environment in which you and your colleagues focus on innovating to improve your library in the future.

Action Step Seven: Focus on impact
This chapter begins with stories about my efforts over many years to encourage the evaluation and assessment of library services, and my three years spent learning about the academic program assessment that is required for a university's accreditation. I focus on three kinds of impact reporting: feedback on service quality, broader ongoing

conversations about community goals, and creating stories to illustrate the library's impact. You will imagine you're Yu Yan, a librarian who creates a new service and receives a video thank-you that will generate support for the project.

As you read the stories and learn about the action steps, bear in mind that libraries are first and foremost human organizations. There are many ways to use this book. You can explore on your own through the stories and takeaways. Think about the advice on changing your approach. Try the activities, especially the ones that bring out your creativity. Find the people in your organization who are driven by passion and mission, and share the ideas in this book with them. Discuss how the action steps can help you create the future you want for your library. Practice the steps that show promise and appeal to you. Adopt the best ones, and assess and improve them. You and your colleagues have the subject matter expertise and imagination to create ways of thinking and working that engage and impact our communities, our customers, employees, and colleagues. Become the innovators and change agents that libraries need in order to thrive.

Notes

1. Michael Gorman, *Our Enduring Values Revisited: Librarianship in an Ever-Changing World* (Chicago: American Library Association, 2015).
2. Susan Orlean, *The Library Book* (New York: Simon and Schuster, 2018), 67.
3. Eric Klinenberg, *Palaces for the People: How Social Infrastructure Can Help Fight Inequality, Polarization, and the Decline of Civic Life* (New York: Broadway Books, 2018), 219–20.

Begin with Yourself

> Everybody has a secret world inside of them. I mean everybody. All of the people in the whole world, I mean everybody—no matter how dull and boring they are on the outside. Inside them they've all got unimaginable, magnificent, wonderful, stupid, amazing worlds . . . Not just one world. Hundreds of them. Thousands, maybe.
> —Neil Gaiman, *A Game of You*

Five months after I became dean of libraries at Georgia Tech, I had the worst surprise of my life. On a quiet Tuesday afternoon before Christmas, I was diagnosed with colon cancer following a routine exam. I had no symptoms. I had no family history. And I had no time to be sick, let alone prepare for long months of treatment and possible death. I was dealing with selling my house and moving from Colorado to Atlanta. I was trying to get to know my colleagues at Georgia Tech and learn about my job. I was fundraising in memory of my father and training for a marathon with a Leukemia & Lymphoma Society team. The timing could not have been worse.

Early in my treatments, I told my oncologist that my father's cancer experience taught me to be more worried about my mental health than my physical recovery. I firmly believed that whether I lived or not would depend on how my body responded to the treatment regime recommended by my doctors, but my attitude, optimism, compassion for myself, and acceptance of kindness from others would determine if and how I came through the terrifying experience. After surgery, I spent 600 hours in chemotherapy over the next six months, and the rest of that year learning about various complementary therapies—mindfulness meditation, guided imagery, acupuncture, and yoga.

My work at the library that year became my refuge from constantly thinking and worrying about the life-threatening illness over which I had no control.

(The Great Recession of 2008–09 and its implications for the library and the university was another constant threat.) My boss and my colleagues were understanding and supportive, if alarmed about what would happen next in my case. I went to work every day during treatment and even managed with Georgia Tech's help to tell my story on-screen for Katie Couric's *CBS News* broadcast about health insurance for colon cancer screening. I wrote a blog for family and friends to keep them up to date, and channel my fears into personal essays. In those months, I learned more about the delicate balance between courage and kindness toward myself and others than I had in sixty years of life.

During that introspective time, I was haunted by the people earlier in my career who had tried to give me advice and feedback that I only partially understood and took to heart. One that sticks with me to this day happened when I was heading up a three-year project to apply 6,000,000 barcodes to the Cornell University Library's collection. I was becoming more and more impatient. Everything that could go wrong was going wrong. My colleagues and I had problems keeping students from quitting because they were bored. We had staff who were tired of training and supervising new employees. We had books without barcodes and barcodes without books. We had librarian colleagues who were supposed to be leading and monitoring progress spending most of their time complaining that the whole project was a waste of time and money. I was annoyed with everyone, and it showed.

After a particularly fractious meeting with my colleagues, my boss hauled me into his office. A father of five and longtime university administrator, he was a master at delivering criticism and stern advice without destroying his listener's will to live another day. He asked me to sit down, leveled his gaze at me, and waited for a very long minute while all I could do was force myself not to jump up and run away.

He spoke slowly and clearly. "You have done an excellent job of leading this project and getting it done as planned. You have all kinds of courage, but sometimes you must slow down and let other people catch up. You go too fast and lose the very people you need to make the changes you want to make." I knew he was right. I was and still am my own worst enemy when it comes to pushing people too hard and fast, for too long. I have lots of passion and plenty of courage, but not enough patience to wait for other people to contribute in their own way and at their own pace. By my actions, I was more interested in distinguishing myself for being courageous than for being kind.

Since then I have received more criticism, most of it less skillfully delivered. In another performance review a few years later, another boss exasperatedly told me that my worst failing was that I was too kind. She was annoyed that I let people get away with behaving badly in order to keep the peace. I had swung from too much courage to too much kindness. In my effort to keep from bulldozing people into doing what I wanted, I had silenced myself. Even now, after cancer and many years of work experience, the delicate balance of courage and kindness is still something of a mystery to me. I have come to terms with accepting that this is my life's work, not a short-term problem to be solved.

Takeaways

The point of telling you about some of the painful times in my life is to encourage you to never stop learning more about yourself. By relating my most cringeworthy moments, I hope to help you avoid similar ones. I know that I may never find the right balance between courage and kindness all the time, but that doesn't prevent me from trying. You will have major and minor challenges of your own, but I have faith in your ability to learn and grow. As an educator, a parent, and a grandparent, I know that we can always improve our way of being in the world.

My path to learning the balance between courage and kindness toward myself and others has had many twists and turns. I was fortunate to have Buddhist friends in Colorado who gave me insights and helpful tools for navigating this self-discovery process. One friend encouraged me to think of slowly climbing a trail on the side of a mountain, where each loop comes back over and over to the same challenges, but every loop is a little bit higher and easier. I also often think of a Buddhist friend's reminder when I repeatedly complained that I was not getting any better at yoga. Every time I would start up my monologue, she would smile beatifically and say, "It is called a 'practice' for a reason." I still rely on a book that the same friend recommended: David Richo's *The Five Things We Cannot Change: And the Happiness We Find by Embracing Them*. I used to have these "five things" written on a card above my desk, and now I carry them in my head—everything changes and ends, things do not always go according to plan, life is not always fair, pain is a part of life, and people are not loving and loyal all the time.[1] I don't see these five things as reasons to quit learning, but as comforts when life and work are not going well.

Although you will want to find your own best ways to learn about yourself, I can offer you a few ways that have helped me. From all the hundreds of hours I have spent in workshops, thousands of hours writing, and tens of thousands of hours reading, I recommend ten activities that have made a difference for me. These activities are suggestions for you to explore, share, practice, apply, and evaluate. Maybe you will incorporate some of them into your life and work, and maybe you won't, but I urge you to experiment with them to find what will work for you.

Reading

This is at the top of my list because like many people who work in libraries, I am a voracious reader. Whenever I want to know anything new, or remember words that helped me in the past, I find something to read to inform and inspire me. Nonfiction, fiction, poetry—it is all there for you to try. One of my favorite parts of working in a library is the opportunity to discuss books with colleagues. You can join book clubs, attend readings and book fairs, sign up for publisher newsletters and websites, and listen to authors tell their stories at conferences. Through other people's stories, you will come into contact with radically different ways of looking at the world that will serve you well as you reimagine library services and collections.

Writing

Communicating clearly and succinctly in writing is a valuable skill to cultivate. When I taught honors program classes at Georgia Tech, I told my students that one of the main advantages of being a reader was becoming a better writer. The more you read, the more you think in phrases and whole sentences that make the process of writing far easier than struggling to come up with one word at a time. Try to find authors and journalists whose style appeals to you, and explore how they express themselves. Practice writing for different audiences and different purposes. Try your hand at writing a "This I Believe" piece for your family and friends to read. Share your writing with your colleagues and ask for encouraging feedback, not brutal criticism. Do the same for them.

Presenting

At conferences and meetings, I'm often struck by the wide variety of presentation skills on display. Some people breeze through their well-crafted presentations with energy and purpose. Others nervously stumble through sharing their thoughts and ideas. Most fall somewhere in between. If speaking to strangers terrifies you, practice will help you overcome those fears. Presenting to your mirror, your cat, or your friends will make your efforts more effective and less stressful. One of the most useful activities that the Colorado State University (CSU) librarians organized when I worked there was lunchtime sessions in which they practiced and kindly critiqued one another before they took the stage at conferences. They not only grew more confident and articulate, but they also improved their teamwork in their own library.

Listening

In this extrovert-focused world, learning to listen to others is a skill that most of us need to improve upon. This fact came home to me during a grueling listening exercise in a mindfulness retreat I attended. After announcing that the next twenty-four hours would be spent in total silence with no reading or electronic devices, the leaders announced that we would spend the following day learning how to listen. For hours on end, we took turns locking eyes and listening to others without responding, and then repeating what we heard. Most of us got better as the day wore on, but we often got lost thinking about what we wanted to say and not hearing what was being said. That we were all exhausted by the effort was proof that most of the time we tune others out. I am better at listening than I used to be, but it will always be a skill that I have to practice. To understand ourselves and be able to hear what others are saying, we need to listen without interrupting, thinking of our response, or piling on tales of our own experiences. To improve your listening skills, ask your family and friends to help, or take a free or low-cost class. Although I am in favor of online learning, building your listening skills works better in person.

Becoming Self-Aware

I have taken several psychometric tests as part of professional workshops, some of them more than once. I find these tests somewhat useful for understanding myself and giving me a lens through which to understand why I work better with some people than others. I disagree with using these tests to determine job performance and workplace fit, but they can be valuable in increasing your self-awareness. What is more valuable is asking for constructive feedback from colleagues, bosses, and friends.

Meditating

Before my cancer diagnosis, one of my colleagues was a Buddhist who recommended formal training in meditation. My first lessons were in the formal Shambhala program at a local community center. Later I was a student at several programs organized by the Massachusetts Medical Center. You can find classes of all kinds offering this training, as well as books, and apps for your phone. Meditation practiced even for short periods on most days is especially helpful in times of great stress, as well as the ordinary day-to-day trials of working and living.

Engaging in Philanthropy

Becoming involved in a charitable cause or program that requires more of oneself than just giving money is a valuable way to learn compassion and generosity. It helps you to get outside the bubble of your own life, even for a short time. Becoming a member of a team devoted to a particular cause also carries over into your team in the workplace. After my father died from lymphoma in 2003, I found a like-minded community in the Leukemia & Lymphoma Society's Team in Training, which helped me deal with all the emotions that came from caring for someone who was mortally ill. I also learned how other people cope with serious problems and manage to maintain their equilibrium.

Expressing Yourself Creatively

My two favorite forms of creative expression are writing and dance. I wish I were a singer or could play a musical instrument. Perhaps you do. There is no better way to learn about what excites and challenges you than to make something and give it to the world. Being able to enjoy theater, art, and music online or in person is an excellent way of learning about yourself—what moves you to laughter or tears, joy or anger, and watching how other people's reactions differ from your own. Every time I am in a museum or art gallery, I think of a student on a six-week Georgia Tech trip through eight cities in Europe. He was sitting on a bench in the Peggy Guggenheim Collection in Paris staring blankly at a piece of modern art. I sat next to him and said nothing. He finally sighed and admitted that he just didn't get whatever he was supposed to get out of the picture. I told him there were no coded messages in paintings; they are what the artists saw or felt when they created them. You, as the viewer, respond however you wish. You might admire the painting technique, the innovation in style, the colors, or the composition. Let yourself feel what the painting makes you feel, which may be nothing at all. What charms or revolts you is unlikely to be exactly the same for someone else, but you can use the experience to understand yourself and others better.

Coaching

Coaching seems like it has become a fad in the workplace, or worse, a code word for paying someone to fix an underperforming employee or an annoying colleague. Regardless of the negative connotations of the word these days, all of us would benefit from coaching—gentle and direct help in working through problems and making better decisions. If you have the opportunity to have a coach or be one, take it. You may be able to find a mentor or a wise friend who is willing to work with you in return for a few cups of coffee, or dinners out. You can structure coaching around a book such as Brene Brown's *Dare to Lead* with your book group, or you can find a coach online. One of the major lessons of my cancer experience is that asking for help is both courageous and kind to yourself.

Get Out and Engage with Other People

Engaging with other people is for me what makes travel joyful and exciting. I often travel by myself. Being an introvert, I sometimes have to force myself to chat with strangers, but I am usually happy that I have taken the time and trouble to do so safely. For years, I have met people all over the world who shared a part of their lives with me and in return taught me about myself. I will never forget the woman near the baggage carousel in Paris who was going on her honeymoon all by herself because her fiancé had canceled their wedding a month before. Or the lone fifteen-year-old who carried my baby daughter in return for my looking after her during a 24-hour delay in Tokyo. Or the three young Italian women who took me on a food tour of Rome and felt like three granddaughters by the end of the evening. If travel is not appealing or an option for you, reading is a good substitute. You can easily be an armchair traveler. There are also countless online travel programs, cooking classes, and other interactive experiences that are inexpensive and informative.

If you are serious about turning outward, you can begin right away to learn more about yourself. Take the time and expend the energy on you. The more self-knowledge and confidence you have, the more compassionate and kinder you will be. With both those qualities brimming over in you, you will have more to offer your friends, family, library, and your community.

Note

1. David Richo, *Five Things We Cannot Change: And the Happiness We Find in Embracing Them* (Boulder, CO: Shambhala, 2006).

Action Step One

Look Outside Your Social Circle, Profession, and Organization for Ideas and Inspiration

> Curiosity takes ignorance seriously and is confident enough to admit when it does not know. It is aware of not knowing, and it sets out to do something about it.
>
> —Alain de Botton, *Art as Therapy*

IN EARLY 2013, I WALKED INTO A CAMPUS AUDITORIUM FOR A MEETING OF Georgia Tech's academic leadership. As the slides about new organizational changes filled the screen, my boss announced that I would manage the university's ten-year accreditation review in addition to my other duties. Later, he cheerfully told me that it was the only time he had ever seen me speechless. This was an understatement. Actually, I'm surprised I didn't have a stroke. This decision was never mentioned to me before that meeting.

I had no previous experience with university-wide accreditation. I had only written compliance reports for three other university libraries in New York, Oregon, and Colorado in three different accreditation regions. I was an amateur, and as I soon found out, not a very gifted one. My learning curve was a straight line upward. I will be forever grateful to the vice-president assigned to Georgia Tech from the Southern Association of Colleges and Schools, Commission on Colleges, for taking pity on me. She helped me learn what I needed to do and avoid making too many mistakes. She saved me from outright humiliation.

For the next two years, several key library employees, including the head of business operations, my assistant, and myself, spent most of our time learning the regional accreditation standards and processes. We organized over 100 people on campus to complete the complicated steps and produce the required compliance reports—600 pages and 2,000 references, plus linked reports.

We managed the off-campus review requirements and set up the on-campus visit, which was like organizing a three-day celebrity event combined with a congressional hearing. Adding to the stress, our review visit coincided with President Obama visiting our campus to talk to Georgia Tech students about financial aid and other higher education issues. Although we didn't realize it as we struggled to get all this work done, our efforts to be good citizens of the university were earning us social credit that would benefit the library in significant ways later.

After years of delay, the renovation of the Georgia Tech Library buildings became a real possibility when the University System of Georgia (USG) reopened its capital construction program in 2012. I was thrilled that we finally had the opportunity to create new designs for the two older library buildings—Price Gilbert and the Crosland Tower—and not be forced to use ten-year-old renovation plans that used compact shelving. Following the rules and regulations from the USG, Georgia Tech architects and construction management offices began choosing an architectural firm. While doing some covert campaigning for inclusion in the project, we held our collective breath waiting to know if we would be included. We were at that dangerous time when the library staff are often relegated to the position of facility users, with only a minor role in designing the buildings.

What saved us from being cut out of the process was the library's social credit with the university architect and others. We had earned those credits by managing the accreditation review and by engaging in pilot projects and user studies that became the inspiration for the Clough Commons (opened 2011), a new classroom and lab building connected to the main library building. The time and energy we spent on these university projects helped convince senior administrators and stakeholders that we could balance our advocacy of the library with the needs of the campus. Unlike our colleagues in many university library renovations, we were rewarded with a seat at the table during the review of the project proposals and the selection of the architectural and the construction management firms.

The challenge for us was how to best take advantage of our involvement in order to influence the redesign of the buildings. We wanted to reimagine the library, not just renovate outdated buildings. We wanted the result to show our commitment to turn our services and collections from inwardly focused to outwardly engaged, from physical to digital, from a book place to a people place.

Over the years of waiting and hoping, I had visited many new and renovated public and academic libraries. Some were beautiful and functional spaces in buildings that cost more than $100 million, while others were on a much smaller scale. I especially appreciated the annual Designing Libraries Conference, which I attended several times at North Carolina State University and the University of Calgary, both of which have exceptional new libraries. Bringing together librarians, architects, and designers to educate and inspire, the conference has created a community that is passionate about rethinking library services and spaces.

At North Carolina State, the University of Calgary, and several new public libraries, I saw ample evidence of the library's changing educational role being incorporated in building designs. In other places, however, I did not see much emphasis on digital services and collections. I did not see flexible designs that could be easily altered in the future. And most important, I did not see spaces that entice people to imagine, learn, and grow. To find more ideas and inspiration, my colleagues and I looked outside the library community altogether. We envisioned the library as a platform for learning and discovery—to demonstrate that libraries are more than big buildings filled with books, study halls, and coffee shops with free Wi-Fi.

Over the next months, we looked at other communities and organizations, for-profit and not-for-profit. And as librarians, of course, we began reading widely. We studied how museums and galleries are using digital tools to encourage virtual visits and interactive experiences. We learned about retail spaces and outdoor exhibits. We visited pop-up shops, restaurants, music venues, coffee bars, technology stores, art exhibits, sports arenas, and even churches. We talked about how the spaces made us feel and what they encouraged us to do, and we watched people all over the world interact with the spaces and with each other.

When we traveled, often dragging family and friends along, we visited museums, national monuments, galleries, theaters, and nonprofits. I spent several hours during a half-marathon weekend in Washington, DC, insisting that my long-suffering family stand in the pouring rain and watch a video wall in a high-end mall near H Street in order to see how the images moved and changed. I parked myself in the National Gallery of Art for hours to watch the digital displays, especially Jenny Holzer's word projections. I begged my family to wait in line for a long time to see the reopening of the Renwick Gallery's display of original art pieces made out of marbles, plastic, embroidery thread, fishing nets, and willow branches, just so I could watch the videos of the artists explaining their work. My preschool granddaughter and I delighted in the digital fish and ocean waves projected on the floor at the American Museum of Natural History's *Unseen Oceans* exhibit (figure 3.1) and other interactive displays.

FIGURE 3.1
Unseen Oceans exhibit at the American Museum of Natural History

One of my colleagues visited the Museum of Science and Industry in Chicago and learned that it hired stand-up comedians from the Second City comedy club as docents. I sought out exhibitions of digital art and children's museums. I attended theater performances in several countries, especially imaginative ones with complex, innovative stage designs. I contacted my colleagues in the botanical garden and natural history museum community to tell me about their efforts to engage the public, especially citizen scientists. We pestered people all over the world to challenge and inspire us.

As well as the firm hired to design the overall architecture and building systems for the renovations, we worked closely with a local architectural firm assigned to the project. Their strong ties to Georgia Tech and their interest in digital technologies helped create a strong learning partnership. We traveled to Boston together to visit a small company that specializes in multimedia displays for museums and galleries. The owner and staff told us about their previous projects and suggested ways that we could incorporate some of their work into the renovated libraries. They later delivered several designs of interactive media, including a media staircase and bridge between the two buildings, which are the basis for media installations planned for the renovated buildings, as funds become available.

With the help of a Massachusetts Institute of Technology faculty member who worked with students to create science museum exhibits and interactive displays, we visited the MIT Museum and a smaller children's science museum. We wanted information about how to create spaces for students and faculty to display their research in ways that would encourage people to learn something they didn't even know they wanted to learn. The highlight of that trip was a visit to Boston's Museum of Science to see the Pixar exhibit. We spent several hours with middle-school students watching them learn about the math and science behind animated movies. We left Boston determined to encourage learning in the library in the same exciting, entertaining ways.

This practice of visiting and engaging others in conversation about what they do and why they do it is deeply ingrained in me. For each of my four library storage facility projects, I visited physically and virtually all kinds of business and organizations—warehouses, manufacturing sites, software firms, theaters, concert halls, and equipment suppliers. I spent so much time in IKEA, Disney World, retail stores, and shopping malls watching people work that it's a wonder I wasn't arrested. I talked to airline employees, hotel managers, coaches, technologists, chefs, dancers, furniture designers, architects, engineers, nonprofit leaders, journalists, doctors, and travel agents—anyone who would tell me about their challenges, solutions, and processes.

My colleagues and I used the same curiosity-satisfying activities to accomplish two other goals for the library transformation—improving our customer service and making our operations more efficient. I was well acquainted with the transition to digital in the book, journal, and newspaper publishing industries and was aware of supply-chain experiments in libraries, especially at the University of Nevada Las Vegas. We decided to go outside of libraries to focus on industry leaders. We studied Amazon and other online retailers and reviewed websites like delta.com for their ability to deliver services at scale.

I especially wanted to learn more about manufacturing organizations that have strong cultures of employee engagement. We took advantage of the skills and experience of some of the members of our team who came from outside the library world. Our consultant from Georgia Tech Strategic Consulting, who had years of experience in the commercial lighting industry, was teaching us how to operate effective project teams, Lean processes, and value chains, but we wanted to see one of these organizations in operation and talk to the employees about their work. Our library's head of facilities and logistics, a former employee of Toyota at their Georgetown, Kentucky, plant, arranged a visit to the plant.

Five of us enthusiastically agreed on a field trip to Georgetown to spend a day at Toyota's massive automotive assembly plant. We all knew about Toyota's reputation for Japanese management practices, especially Lean manufacturing, and we were anxious to learn how they encouraged employee engagement and productivity. Early in the morning on the day of our visit we arrived at the plant, suited up in our long pants, shirts with sleeves, and closed toe shoes, just like our colleagues at Georgia Tech who work in labs and construction sites. We put on our required gear—glasses, vests, and hard hats—as our hosts explained the safety requirements of the plant.

I had visited mining sites and oil refineries with my father, along with dozens of warehouses and other industrial buildings while working on library storage, but I was unprepared for the size and the noise when we walked out of the visitors' center into the assembly plant. We got there at the start of the first shift in order to observe the morning meeting. We watched from the sidelines as supervisors and team leaders gathered in a room filled with whiteboards and charts. Each manager reported on their area of responsibility, pointing out productivity, delays, problems, and successes. Everyone in the room was attentive and respectful while their colleagues spoke. There was no grandstanding or side conversations. People walked around the room and read the graphics that showed the state of the plant.

As we made our way carefully behind our tour guide into the main body of the plant, we did our best to follow the safety rules—stay in line, walk only in designated areas, and signal direction at corners to ensure that drivers and wire-guided carts had priority. We watched robotic welding on screens above the chambers. We observed employees at work on the assembly line putting together dashboards and doors. We learned about the steps in the manufacturing process—stamping metal, welding, and on through the assembly line. We visited the ergonomic section to try out the exercises, which determine what kinds of jobs someone will do on the line. Short people like me, for example, are not given tasks that require them to constantly stretch their hands over their head to grab a part or a tool. Employees rotate around jobs frequently in order to avoid repetitive motion injuries. Keeping the assembly line safely moving is everyone's chief goal and responsibility.

To ensure Lean manufacturing and the elimination of wasteful processes, Toyota encourages input from employees to improve productivity and safety. We learned about high-impact changes to the assembly line suggested by employees. One of these was implementing parallel assembly lines for doors and chassis so that it was easier for employees to work inside the car bodies without damaging the doors. We were shown large team whiteboards where they recorded their training, issues, concerns, and goals. As we left the plant, our heads were full of ideas about how to encourage input and take full advantage of people's skills and knowledge, and at the same time keep the library moving forward. We left with ringing ears and new ideas.

Takeaways

The purpose of these stories is to encourage you to find ways to learn from individuals and organizations outside the library. The people and places you visit or read about may not inspire you to adopt their ideas, but they will reward your curiosity and enhance your desire to keep learning. My former university librarian at Cornell, a professor of eighteenth-century French literature, actor, and master fundraiser, taught me that we all have filters about family members, friends, and colleagues. We say, "Oh, Jane always says that. Jim always wants to solve a problem that way. Pete always laughs at the wrong time when he gets nervous." Because we try to keep ourselves safe, we often screen out what we find frightening—new ideas, new people, and new experiences. We are pattern thinkers who constantly compare and contrast the information that is going through our brains with what we already know. We have a bias for the familiar, the predictable. Consequently, we have to be aware of our filters, which prevent us from listening to new ideas and ways of working, and we have to try constantly to overcome them. Even if you are not redesigning a building or making substantial changes in workflows, you will learn by engaging others in conversation, listening to their ideas, and asking questions.

For some of my colleagues, this kind of engaging others by asking questions does not come easily. It may be the same for you. If like me you are naturally an introvert, I highly recommend learning about "informational interviewing," which is a technique for people who are trying to decide what kind of job and field they want. In such an interview, a person who is investigating a career or workplace asks questions of someone who is already working in that field or workplace. In these interviews, the potential candidate asks questions such as "What is it like to work in this field? What is your typical day like? What do you enjoy most about your job? What do you enjoy least?"

I first learned about informational interviewing from the book *What Color Is Your Parachute?* and was struck by how useful the technique could be for information gathering for all kinds of purposes. At Georgia Tech, when I taught a special topics class in the honors program called "The Literature of Livelihood: Reading and Writing about Work," we used the informational interview technique to learn about why people chose their work and what they liked about it, or not. As informational interviewers, most of the students needed help identifying contacts and needed practice in asking strangers questions and listening carefully to their answers. After their formal class presentations, the students reported that they had sharpened their curiosity, listening, and storytelling skills.

Informational interviewing can be used to learn about organizations and ideas as well as new career paths. The process is effective, but it takes some courage and preparation. You need a referral or a contact in a job, field, or organization that interests you. If you need help making a contact, ask your colleagues, family members, and friends. Once you have a name, send them a polite note asking for thirty minutes of their time to talk with you. Reassure them that you don't expect them to hire you, or to become your mentor. Prepare a short statement to tell the person who you are and what you want to know. People are usually generous with short amounts of their time as long as you make it clear that all you want is information for a particular purpose. If they don't have the time or the interest, they probably will refuse. Thank them for their consideration and move on.

Here is a story that might give you some ideas. Imagine you are a librarian named Jenny who works in a small-town library, located outside of a major metropolitan area. You are friends with several doctors and nurses at the hospital in town who are worried by the increasing rates of type 2 diabetes, especially in younger people. They consult the local public health department and other city organizations—including the library—looking for ideas. You suggest that the library offer programs that will help people understand nutrition and how it impacts health. You have heard that some public libraries have cooking classes, and you want to find out if you can offer a fun, educational event at the library with both a public health nurse and a local chef. You are excited about the possibility of finding books to recommend and even offering guided shopping trips to the local supermarket. You have a good idea and enthusiasm, but wonder if the event is feasible given the library's tight budget.

You have a friend, Anne, who knows a librarian who works for an urban library as the cooking librarian. You ask Anne to introduce you to this librarian, Sarah, who says she would be delighted to talk to you. She loves her job and wants to see more cooking programs in libraries all over the country. You set up time for a call. Meanwhile, you go online and find out what you can about cooking classes in libraries and cooking librarians. You also call the local chapter of the National Diabetes Association and ask to speak to one of their information specialists.

When it's time for your phone call with Sarah, you have your interview questions ready. You want to ask Sarah what her program is like, in the short time you have with her. You start off by explaining your idea. Then you ask Sarah for her opinion about the idea and what it would take to make it work. At the end of the call, you thank her for her time and ask if you could send her an e-mail if you have another question or two. Sarah not only agrees, but also invites you to her library if you want to see her cooking program in action. You schedule a call to talk to Julie at the National Diabetes Association chapter office in your state, and then you call your doctor friend, Kelly, to ask if any of the local chefs might be willing to talk to you.

As you can tell from this example, informational interviewing takes a few contacts, a bit of courage, and time to prepare and engage others, but it is an effective way to learn from people outside your library and your community. By turning yourself outward, you are turning your library toward your community.

Shift Your Approach

FROM	TO
Sticking with familiar people and places	Seeking new people and experiences
Relying on what you already know	Pursuing new knowledge
Ignoring your biases and fixed options	Being aware of your limiting perspectives
Spending time only in your library	Learning about other workplaces and communities
Turning yourself inward	Engaging with others

Activities

1. Explore how your insights about yourself help improve your interactions with others.
2. Share your time with others and encourage them to share their knowledge about other professions, workplaces, and organizations.
3. Practice conducting informational interviews to learn about people in other fields and other generations.
4. Apply the ideas and strategies you learn from other people and organizations to your own situation.
5. Evaluate with your colleagues how well your new ways of thinking and working are helping you and your library.

Action Step Two
Be Curious about the Future

"You will be fine," the fortune-teller says. "There may be decisions to make and surprises in store. Life takes us to unexpected places sometimes. The future is never set in stone, remember that."
—Erin Morgenstern, *The Night Circus*

I**N 2010 WE WERE COMING OUT OF THE GREAT RECESSION, BUT WE WERE** mindful of how quickly our world was changing. The present was not what we expected, and we tried not to think about what the future would bring. We were waiting, but we were not sure why. I call it a "holding our breath" time. The Association of Research Libraries' (ARL's) scenarios project started right when I needed it.

Because it is aware that most planning in libraries is not strategic but tactical, the ARL set out to encourage libraries to stop thinking about the future as a continuation of the present. The scenarios project urged us to use stories to imagine different futures, some appealing and some not, in which we would work and live. Building scenarios offered us a way to stop being afraid to imagine what was coming next and enjoy speculating about what could be. As a lifelong reader of fiction, I was intrigued and jumped at the opportunity to participate in the project.

The other members of the project committee and I spent days in training and brainstorming sessions taught by a consultant with extensive experience at Royal Dutch Shell. Shell was a pioneer in scenario development outside of the military more than fifty years ago and continues to promote its value to this day. Many different kinds of for-profit and nonprofit organizations use various forms of scenario planning to anticipate and plan for the future.

I learned that the Shell process is to create stories, not forecasts, about possible futures that are plausible and not too challenging. These stories, or "scenarios," have data but are not based on mathematical models. I like to think of scenarios in the original meaning of the word from the commedia dell'arte—brief sketches tacked to the back of the scenery in the playhouse to give the actors the basic plot, but not all the details and dialogue. The actors know when they are supposed to be on stage and what actions they must perform to move the story forward. For all the rest, they improvise. The closest analogy to theater scenarios today is improvisational comedy, in which the actors only have the basic idea or question, and then they take it from there by improvising.

When done well, scenario planning builds speed and creativity in thinking and expression. The purpose is not to develop strategies, since most of the scenarios are unlikely to play out as written, but to sharpen our wits and lessen our fear of the future. By carefully considering the current environment and forcing ourselves to imagine alternative futures, we can improve our capacity to handle whatever challenges come along.

As the authors of the workbook *The ARL 2030 Scenarios: A User's Guide for Research Libraries* note in the introduction: "Confronting uncertainty in a rapidly changing environment is essential. . . 'wait and see' is appealing, but [it] exposes libraries to the risks of irrelevance and replacement. By delaying decision-making, we may magnify the risks to our organization's future instead of reducing them."[1]

The ARL's project created four scenarios about university-based research. The planning sessions were about the future of research and researchers in 2030, not about libraries and how they would function. We wanted to encourage the member libraries of ARL to use the scenarios and the workbook as a conversation starter, a way for us all to sharpen our skills at anticipating the future, without narrowing the focus to libraries too soon.

I was fascinated by the techniques of scenario planning. We began by defining what our instructor called "critical uncertainties" in the research environment of North American research universities. We created a 2 × 2 grid. On one axis we put individual researchers, and on the other axis we put the research enterprise. We created four scenarios, one in each of the four squares in the grid. We were warned not to create a chronology of change in which one scenario would lead to another over time. We settled on four distinct pictures of what the university research environment would look like in twenty years, calling these scenarios Research Entrepreneurs, Reuse and Recycle, Global Followers, and Disciplines in Charge (see figure 4.1).

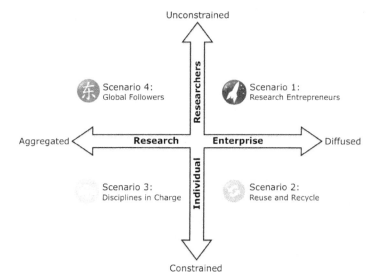

FIGURE 4.1
ARL 2030 Scenarios

The ARL staff and consultants wrote a separate story for each scenario populated by a fictional researcher named Hannah Chen and her colleagues. Each scenario described an alternative future for these characters. The project team also gathered the scenarios into a workbook that includes an end-state table for 2030, advice on mapping out the planning process, and guidance on hosting workshops that creatively engage the organization and keep the conversation going.[2]

The ARL scenario set and the workbook were thought-provoking and powerful tools, but the research library community definitely was not ready to take them seriously in 2010. In one workshop I attended, those deans and directors who had more practice with techniques such as writing use cases and disaster planning were able to get into the spirit of the discussion. Others, however, rejected the scenarios that they disliked or thought were implausible; they preferred to concentrate on their favorite happy ending. Others wanted to rewrite the scenarios on a timeline: first this one happened, and then another one and another one. Some wanted to ignore the future altogether and focus on their most pressing issues, such as when funding lost in the Great Recession would be restored. They made it clear that they had no time and interest in chatting about made-up futures.

I found the same resistance when I brought the four scenarios back to Georgia Tech. The librarians and the library's Faculty Advisory Board members tried to get on board, but they had the same difficulties as some of the deans and directors in the workshop. I tried for several months to persuade the vice-president for research to host a workshop for university faculty, to ask them how they and their colleagues would respond to the four versions of the future. I wanted the library to apply what we had learned in the workshop to making decisions about how to support faculty members in the future. The vice-president listened to my pitch, but never followed up. I could not fault him for thinking that the immediate issues of the day were too serious to ask researchers to spend time on "what if" discussions. The faculty members were too busy building research programs and competing for grants to have theoretical conversations about becoming research rock stars.

Three years later, when the renovation of the library became a real possibility, we didn't have faculty members' insight into the future of research and learning, nor did we have well-developed scenario-planning skills to guide us. Instead, we had to begin gathering intelligence about where the university's research and teaching were going in the future. We debated hiring a consultant to help us conduct ethnographic studies like the University of Rochester had done, but we didn't have time for long-term reflection and study. We needed to align the building renovation design to new services because the building project was moving forward.

Since we were determined to have a library redesign that would be functional as well as beautiful, three of the senior librarians set out to find a consulting firm to fast-track our intelligence-gathering from the faculty and the students. We didn't want the consulting firm to come to campus, conduct focus groups, and then hand us a plan. We wanted them to teach us to interview faculty members about how they work and how their work is changing. We wanted to engage the community in structured conversations about the future of research and learning in order to inform the design of the renovated buildings, thereby creating flexible and adaptable spaces. We didn't want our successors on the library staff to struggle as we have with work and study areas that are expensive and time-consuming to alter as research and learning change in unpredictable ways.

We and our consultants conducted a study in two parts. The first part focused on understanding the research, teaching, and learning on campus. The second part identified service and space opportunities based on campus needs in order to inform the renovation design process, as well as future staffing and service models. The consultants, in collaboration with the user research task force, interviewed faculty members and leaders in the colleges and schools, conducted observations of spaces on campus, and hosted workshops. Their findings became the first report. Later, a second report on user engagement and specific design work offered insights about how research and learning are changing, and proposed a user experience model of five goals that people are trying to achieve—discovering, focusing, growing, creating, and showcasing. Together the Georgia Tech Library and the consultants created a playbook of how to implement the guiding principles--integrate in one place, connect physical and digital, enable flow, meet people where they are, be agile, be neutral, make things visible, be a platform, and reach out to users.[3]

Although the ideas behind the library renovation project were based on an eighteen-month process that sought to discover the goals and aspirations of the community, to this day I worry about how to keep the campus conversation going now that the buildings have been completed. Without purposeful, ongoing conversations with users, the library won't be able to adapt and change effectively over time. We need a way of endlessly re-creating the playbook, otherwise we will be stuck forever in the past. We don't want to repeat what some other libraries have done—opening a renovated library and then ceasing to think about continuous change.

I never stopped looking for ways to focus on the future beyond the time when the libraries reopened. I wanted to set up an ongoing conversation with faculty and students about the future of learning and research and how the library could support those efforts, but when Crosland Tower reopened in 2019, the campus was in the thick of a complex political situation that impacted everyone. People had no available time and energy to focus on the library or its future. I had to wait and look for other ways to raise the issue after more time had passed. As often happens in the world of work, the present crisis was crowding out the future.

A few months later, I read about the American Library Association's relationship with the Harwood Institute to sponsor training sessions called the Harwood Public Innovators Lab for Libraries, and the next workshop would be held in Atlanta. Public libraries are the usual focus of this training, but two of my colleagues and I signed up, hoping to learn about the Harwood process of what they call "turning the library outward toward the community," and what we called "moving from a fortress to a platform."

The workshop in Atlanta was filled with public librarians from large and small institutions, a few academic librarians like us, and many United Way employees from South Carolina. Over three days we learned the Harwood process, which focuses on two interconnected roles for the library. Through focus group conversations within the community, hosted by the library, participants are asked about their aspirations for their community.

There are three main questions in these community conversations. "What are your aspirations for your community? How far is the community from achieving those aspirations? What might be done to achieve those aspirations?" In this part of the process, the library becomes what I think of as a future-facing archivist, recording the answers, summarizing them, and giving them back to the community. From this summary of the community conversations, the library decides on its own path forward. It does not ask the community members what they want from the library, but instead works out the role it will play in the achievement of the community's aspirations, and what partners it will need to make a difference. Harwood calls this turning the library toward listening, not telling, and asking, not assuming or directing.[4]

My colleagues and I felt that we had finally found some allies in the library community for what we were seeking to accomplish. The Harwood Institute used a similar vocabulary to the one we were already using. We were impressed by the similarities between Harwood's process and the one we had learned from our consulting firm. Although we were already trying to steer away from problems, wishes, and complaints toward other, more positive outcomes, we valued the techniques and the insights from the workshop leader and other attendees about how to be more effective. Most importantly, we learned that we need to use our subject matter expertise to drive the library forward after we listen, not before. This distinction is subtle but crucial.

Takeaways

I have told you this story to encourage you to be curious about the future in an organized and purposeful way. Often in our library lives and our personal lives, we are so busy and worried about the present that we have no time or energy left over for anything else. We rush from one day to the next, fixing problems and dealing with crises. All this is understandable in an uncertain world, but fearing the future, instead of looking forward to it, is neither healthy nor desirable.

I am making the case that being curious about the future will help you move forward confidently. If you have the time and resources to learn and apply techniques such as simulation games, scenario planning, and playbook development, you will benefit from engaging your mind and exercising your imagination. If you want to focus more on public knowledge than on expert knowledge, you might try organizing conversations about the future with small groups of people in your library or community.

You can always start small as you practice elevating your sights from today toward a future that excites you. You will build confidence in your ability to plan and to change your plans as needed. Think of this as creative writing or acting for a purpose. Seek out people who know about improvisational comedy and ask them to help you. Write a few case studies and get people debating them. Propose some possible and some wacky future scenarios and talk about them with anyone who wants to participate.

34 / Chapter 4

Here is an exercise I have used for my own planning that will give you the idea. All you need is a free hour or two, a large piece of paper, and a marker. You can write it on your laptop if that works better for you. A flare for storytelling and drama helps but is not required. Think of a problem you need to solve. Write down ten ways you could solve it that do not repeat. Pick four of them. Draw four quadrants on the page. Write one solution in each space—for this exercise it doesn't matter which one is in which square. Write a short description of each option with you as the main character. Remember that the options do not have to be mutually exclusive. Most solutions turn out to be combinations. Have fun.

Imagine you are Pat, a branch manager at an urban public library. The library is charged with writing a plan for how it will engage more often with the community as part of a city-wide library effort, and the deadline for this report is only one month away. Moreover, everyone in the library is scrambling to keep operations going after two key staff members were transferred to other branches. Everyone wants to be more involved with the community, but they don't know how to accomplish this. They need good ideas right away to get this report done on time. The pressure is on. The annual budget conversations are starting downtown, and the mayor is definitely not a library supporter. Here are the four principal options, one in each quadrant:

Pat closes his office door and starts writing.	Everyone has a meeting to pick two projects.
Pat calls the central library and asks for more time.	Everyone comes together to host focus groups with community members.

- Option: You close the office door and begin writing.

    You are feeling desperate and you want to submit a plan on time, but constant interruptions to solve problems are not helping. The library is so short-staffed that no one else can take the time to work on the plan. Everyone is surprised to see a "Do Not Disturb" sign on your office door, but they shrug and keep working. You stare at the screen and think about what you can possibly propose to do that would engage the community. A problem from a few months ago comes to mind: people in the community need books in Spanish and Russian. That's

Action Step Two: Be Curious about the Future / 35

it! After checking on what other libraries have done to acquire more Spanish- and Russian-language books, you start typing furiously.

- Option: You call the central library and ask for more time.

    You hate this idea. It would embarrass you and everyone in the library and not get the plan written. It would be a missed opportunity that everyone would regret. You all want to engage with the community, but the problem is that you are struggling to get work done and still think about the future at the same time. You call colleagues at other branches to find out how writing the planning document is going for them. Everyone else has either finished their plan or will have it done before the deadline. Then another disaster strikes: a water leak over the bank of computers caused by broken air-conditioning is dripping all over the equipment and furnishings. You slump back into the office to call the HVAC repair service, and then you call the director of the central library to plead for more time.

- Option: Everyone has a meeting in order to pick two projects.

    While you are worrying about how to satisfy the central library, one of the librarians suggests calling a meeting of the entire branch to figure out what to do. Although you know the library is in tune with users, it does not have deep ties to their rapidly changing part of the city. There are more frequent clashes between older adults and teens over noise and computers in the afternoons, and more young children are accompanied by caregivers, not parents. On the day of the meeting, everyone starts out focusing on all the problems, but you ask them to try to think about solutions. You all spend two hours in the small windowless conference room listing your ideas on big sheets of paper with sticky notes. Everyone decides on one idea to help with the teens versus adults issue, and another for the story time issue. Everyone expresses their worry that each solution that has been proposed might actually make the problem worse, but they don't know what else to do.

- Option: Everyone comes together to host focus groups with key members of the community.

    At a stand-up morning meeting, you tell everyone about the plan that is due in a month at the central library. Everyone talks about some of the problems the library is having, but they agree that they don't know if those are the most important ones. Two librarians offer to work with you to make a list of community members and call them to ask them to attend one of three focus groups scheduled for the following week. Staff members put out a call for participants on the website and a sign on the door inviting people to come. They offer the option of participating online if that is more convenient. They decide who will be the facilitator and who will be the scribe. They agree that they are going to focus on solutions, not problems. After the meeting, one of the librarians summarizes what people told them and posts it on the library's website and sends the notes to everyone who attended. The good news is that they not only started engaging the community, but they have two ideas for the future. You write a short report outlining how everyone helped by seeking community input, working on the plan to keep the conversation going, and identifying the two issues they want to address with the community in the coming months.

The last two options remind us that it takes discipline and courage to turn outward when you want to turn inward. Being curious about the future is enjoyable the more you do it. The agency and preparedness that come from these speculative activities are worth the effort. Future-facing conversations build the muscle we will need to make it through the endurance event that is called work-life. By engaging others in gathering information and making decisions, you are turning yourself and your library toward your community.

Shift Your Approach

FROM	TO
Focusing on short-term problems	Being curious about the future
Avoiding speculating and forecasting	Considering different outcomes
Hoping for the best	Planning for whatever might happen
Engaging in magical thinking	Seeking information and evidence
Avoiding making decisions	Making timely decisions

Activities

1. Explore different future-facing techniques and strategies.
2. Share your curiosity about the future with your colleagues.
3. Practice ways of preparing for the future with techniques such as the four-square grid and writing stories.
4. Apply what you have learned to create a playbook of different futures for your library.
5. Evaluate your plans for the future by comparing them to what actually happened.

Notes

1. Association of Research Libraries and Stratus Inc., *The ARL 2030 Scenarios: A User's Guide for Research Libraries* (Washington, DC: Association of Research Libraries, 2010), 7.
2. Association of Research Libraries and Stratus Inc., "The ARL 2030 Scenarios: A User's Guide for Research Libraries," www.arl.org/wp-content/uploads/2010/01/arl-2030-scenarios-users-guide.pdf.
3. Georgia Institute of Technology and brightspot strategy, "User Research Project: Part 1: Research Report & Playbook," 2014, www.library.gatech.edu/sites/default/files/2019-01/part1.pdf; Georgia Institute of Technology and brightspot strategy, "Service Design Overview," 2014, https://library.gatech.edu/sites/default/files/2019-01/GT-Library-Service-Design-Overview.pdf.
4. Harwood Institute for Public Innovation, "Public Innovators Lab Guide," Bethesda, Maryland, 2017 (unpublished).

Action Step Three
Make Bold, Public Plans

> Do stuff. Be clenched, curious. Not waiting for inspiration's shove or society's kiss on your forehead.
> —Susan Sontag

As the U.S. economy teetered on the brink of collapse in August 2008, I became dean of libraries at Georgia Tech. The warning signs had been evident for months, but when Lehman Brothers abruptly shut its doors in mid-September after 150 years in business, widespread economic panic set in. And meanwhile, the good-faith promises about the library renovation which had been made to me when I was a candidate were never mentioned now. My colleagues and I spent that autumn trying to work out how to cut collections and services without laying off library employees. For the next eighteen months, all capital construction projects in the University System of Georgia were on hold, the collections budget shrank by 10 percent, employees were furloughed, and hiring was frozen.

From 2008 until 2010 we were in survival mode. With help from our Georgia State University Library colleagues, we worked out an online method to solicit input from the faculty about which journal subscriptions to cut. I brought RAPID Interlibrary Loan to Georgia Tech, and recruited other research libraries in the Southeast to mitigate the effects of the serials cuts on faculty and students. We didn't have the staff or the money to update the library's services, but we kept pressing for funds to finish the third small renovation project—which my predecessor had made possible—by temporarily moving more of the collection to an off-campus storage facility.

As the economy strengthened, the USG and Georgia Tech returned to their ambitious plan to attach a new classroom and lab building to the main library building. We envisioned a 220,000-square-foot structure, now called the G. Wayne Clough Undergraduate Learning Commons, to house various academic services, as well as first-year science labs and classrooms. Because many of the new services incorporated into the building had been piloted in the three small renovation projects in the library, the university architect and his colleagues welcomed library staff into the design process.

After twelve years of on-again, off-again planning and construction, Clough Commons opened in August 2011. Seven months before the grand opening, the library was abruptly given the responsibility for managing the new facility. It was not quite as much of a shock to me as becoming responsible for the campus reaccreditation process, but it was an unwelcome surprise nevertheless. Although the decision made sense because Clough Commons is physically connected to the main library building, it should have been made months earlier. We didn't have close relationships with the academic departments moving into the building, and no one had resources to spare. Although I was worried that we would fail, I'd had enough experience with crisis operations to just grit my teeth and get started.

I was told to work with a university planner who had been assigned by campus leadership. She had not worked on the design or construction of the new building, but she had well-developed university project management skills. We were told to start with a large spreadsheet of hastily assembled operating cost estimates. After I got over the shock and we set to work, I quickly realized that securing staffing and funding for operations and maintenance on short notice would stretch the already overworked library staff even more. With our planners' help and support, I persuaded the university to upgrade three senior library positions—for logistics, facilities, and security—and I asked for a modest number of new staff and student employees to ensure that the new building was safe and well-managed for 24-hour operations.

In the weeks leading up to the opening of Clough Commons, we scrambled to send our logistics staff to safety training to learn how to handle chemicals and other shipments for the labs. We reorganized our library's security services to cover twice as much space and remain open twenty-four hours a day, seven days a week. We worked with campus facilities personnel to sort out the unfinished construction issues. We partnered with technology staff to work out all the digital signage and support services for users and staff in Clough Commons. When the building opened its doors a few days before the beginning of the fall semester, we were ready with tours, signage, and events.

After successfully planning and opening Clough Commons, the library had a stockpile of good citizenship credit with Georgia Tech's leadership. Happily, we turned our attention back to our first love, the library. I decided we needed a public plan to encourage everyone to focus on the library's future, and I wanted to keep the dream of a renovation alive. I knew it was going to be a hard sell now that Clough Commons had taken the pressure off, and the state and national economies were still shaky.

As I look back, I realize that I was fueled by great frustration and a growing sense of desperation. I had arrived at Georgia Tech in 2008, worried about the impact of the housing market's collapse on the U.S. economy, but hopeful that the library's outstanding work in updating spaces and services would continue. I wanted to make sure that the culture of innovation for which the library had won the Association of College and Research Libraries' Library of the Year Award did not die on my watch.

By late 2011, I had grown tired of waiting for a major renovation of the library. I was impatient with how slowly we were focusing leadership's attention on the pressing need for a library that matched the reality and the ambitions of Georgia Tech as a global university. I was worried that we would lose our credit for being good stewards of resources and good citizens of the university if too much time passed without a renovation. And I was increasingly annoyed by how often we were dismissed as old-fashioned librarians with out-of-date ideas about what students and faculty members need. Moreover, we were losing talented librarians who wanted to keep innovating. The clock was ticking.

As a self-proclaimed disrupter, I knew it was time to act. We had a window of opportunity that could close at any time, and we had social credit that could soon expire. We had to do something dramatic and we had to do it soon. The two library buildings, the Price Gilbert Memorial Library (occupied in 1953) and the adjacent Dorothy M. Crosland Tower (opened in 1968), were crumbling. Keeping the buildings functioning cost the university more than $500,000 a year to repair or replace worn-out building systems. Electrical and plumbing problems were a constant hazard. Water intrusion caused by storms and broken pipes, and subsequent mold outbreaks plagued us.

Our most politically acceptable path forward was to propose a renovation of the buildings rather than a replacement. The Price Gilbert Library has four floors of mostly open public space, plus a roof penthouse, basement, and sub-basement. Designed by the Atlanta architect and Georgia Tech professor M. Paul Heffernan, Price Gilbert is regarded as a jewel of mid-century modern design and is on the list of protected buildings on campus. It is an open, light-filled structure with gracious proportions and classic 1950s design elements. But by 2012, after nearly sixty years of operation, its building systems were failing, and some spaces could no longer be used by the public or the staff.

Before it reopened in 2019, Crosland Tower was a brick-clad silo designed to store books. There were seven-foot ceilings over a core of book stacks on every windowless floor except the first, which had been partially renovated in 2006. The building was a dark and depressing place for people. Students desperate for places to study crammed themselves into carrels in corners, and library staff worked in former closets and makeshift spaces carved out of the edges of the stacks. Lighting, power, and data were available but inadequate to meet demand.

I came to Georgia Tech with a deep dislike of compact shelving and multiple service desks, which I considered relics of the time when preservation of the collection was more important than offering outstanding library services. I rejected the reports and renovation blueprints from 2007, which were based on out-of-date ways of providing services and managing the collections. I wanted a bold new renovation plan for the two buildings that would fit the culture of Georgia Tech and focus on the future, not the past.

I assembled a small group of employees who knew the history of the campus and the library as well as the condition of the buildings. They were the people who on a daily basis had to deal with problems, provide services, and manage the collections to keep the library operating. The head of library facilities and the librarian most knowledgeable about the physical collection led our data-gathering effort, and together with a few others, we worked out our strategy to secure attention and support.

In fourteen pages of minimal text and well-chosen facts, photos, floor plans, and charts, our report, "Library 2020," issued a bold challenge to the busy administrators, scientists, and engineers who make up Georgia Tech's senior leadership. In its pages we walked them through the brief history and current use of each building. We included grim photos of mechanical spaces and depressing stack areas to focus their attention on our challenge to the university (see figure 5.1).

Action Step Three: Make Bold, Public Plans / 43

Judge S. Price Gilbert Memorial Library
Architect: Bush-Brown, Gailey and Heffernan
Construction Cost: $1,881,000
Year Occupied: 1953
Gross Square Feet: 99,832
Assignable Square Feet: 63,698

FIGURE 5.1
"Georgia Tech Library 2020" report

We boldly promised to reduce the footprint of book stacks from 46 percent to 24 percent of assignable space, a 52 percent reduction in the volumes held on campus. We also committed to purchasing all journals in electronic form and shrinking significantly the government document collection, maps, and microforms. In return, we asked Georgia Tech to address the serious life-safety problems in the deteriorating buildings.

Not content to let another space plan gather dust, we organized tours for Georgia Tech's executive leadership, faculty members, student advisory boards, and anyone else we could entice into listening to us. We showed people the aging HVAC systems, the corroded pipes, the water-damaged stairways, and the dark, scary parts of the buildings.

While leading our guests up and down narrow staircases to bathrooms with broken tiles and 60-year-old HVAC systems, we talked about how the buildings were a constant source of anxiety, especially for those who worked the third shift in the middle of the night. While we walked, our head of facilities reported on minor electrical fires, asbestos problems, and damaged books due to mold outbreaks in the basement. The rest of us chimed in about the absence of sprinklers, the aging fire alarm systems, and poor disability access. We pointed out the worn, rarely used books and journals taking up prime campus real estate and bragged about how students and faculty were returning to the few renovated spaces in Crosland and Price Gilbert. We loudly expressed our fears about not being able to safely evacuate students in an emergency, especially in the middle of the night. We did not just say the words "life-safety"; we showed them why we were afraid. Stunned by the deteriorating buildings and aware of their heavy use day and night, our champions, especially the executive vice-president for administration and finance, emerged from the tours ready to rally to the cause.

After almost a year of tours and presentations but no concrete conversations about funding, we refused to give up hope. My experience during the Great Recession counseled me to take the long view. We knew that large public organizations move slowly, and support for change funded with public money is hard to secure. Years before, I learned from a group of women leaders at Cornell when we were trying to get support for an infant day care center that the best strategy is "the dripping water method," meaning don't go away until someone either fixes the problem or gives you the money to fix it yourself.

So we kept on touring, talking, and issuing our bold challenge. When the USG finally reopened discussions about capital construction, the executive leadership team at Georgia Tech rushed to put the library buildings on the system-wide list as our university's highest priority and began working with USG administrators, state political leaders, and legislators to secure funding to renew the buildings for another sixty years.

By challenging ourselves to think creatively about what we could offer in exchange for support, we got the university's attention. We were not begging or whining; we were offering to be part of the solution. Despite the economy's slow recovery from the Great Recession, we did not give into despair; we created a plan that we would promote until opportunity knocked. We had no clear ideas about how or where we were going to move all the books or how we would afford an all-digital collection, but we did promise to obtain these things.

We intentionally shocked leaders and members of the community with how bad the conditions in the buildings were, and we gave voice to our fears for the safety of students, faculty, and staff for whom we felt responsible. We picked the most dramatic photos and tour routes. Best of all, we worked together to articulate to the world what we wanted and what we were willing to do to get it. Even if champions and supporters were taking a long time to convince, we still had a bold plan and the fortitude to keep moving forward.

Later, during the design process for the renovations, we used the skills we had developed creating bold plans in order to seek partnerships for mutual benefit. Georgia Tech's collaboration with Emory University to create a shared collection and build the Library Service Center solved our problem of high-quality storage space for the collections of older books and journals, and the new facility offers students and faculty access to research materials they need, especially in the social sciences and humanities. The architects, designers, and facilities units at Georgia Tech and the two architectural firms generously allowed us to be deeply involved in all aspects of the renovation designs. With the services of an experienced consulting firm, we reached out to the community and made choices about how we wanted our library services to be in the future. In meeting after meeting and event after event, we showed the plans and asked for feedback and were rewarded with information we used to better serve the community.

Takeaways

The purpose of this story is to encourage you to be creative and bold in making your plans, but not to make them alone. The most important first step is to gather intelligence from your colleagues about past plans that the library put forward, especially if you are new to the organization. Remember that most plans are modest in scope, not major building renovations. Try not to get discouraged or bogged down in the old plans' details, but to understand why you may be told, "We tried that before, and it didn't work." After your brief survey of the past, you can set to work learning about the present and thinking creatively about the future.

This is the time to go outside the library to your community—not to ask what you can do for them, but to find out who they are and what success looks like to them. If you are in a university, people may want to shorten the time it takes them to earn a degree. If you are in a city, people may want a safe place to raise their children. If you are in a special library, people may want to get their work done more efficiently. Your goal is to figure out what you, your colleagues, and the library as a whole can do to help further other people's goals. As one of my friends likes to say, "You are not Luke Skywalker, you are Obi-Wan Kenobi—the guide, not the hero of this story."

When you know what the community wants, and what the library can realistically offer, it is time to write your plan. Then you take it on the road, looking for partners who are allies, not just supporters or funders. It may take time for you to build honest and open relationships with the individuals and groups that you identify. Building trust and credibility are vital. Along the way, you will have to make some choices and adjust your plans to reality. Like we did, you might have to make some choices that are hard for you. You might have to give up something, in order to get something you want more. You might decide to trade a space to get another better space, or take responsibility for more events in order to get marketing help from a communications expert. You might, as we did, offer to move books out of the library to make more room for people.

Once you and your colleagues have worked out your most important goals, made your hard choices, and created your partnerships, you need to make your revised plan public. That is the signal to the community that the library has heard what the community wants and is enthusiastically committed to

Action Step Three: Make Bold, Public Plans / 47

updating itself to meet changing needs. Your plan must be written in simple, direct language and include visual materials. Pictures really are worth a thousand words. And don't be shy about stating your case dramatically.

When you have what you want to say ready, you have many choices for how to send it into the world. Enlist your partners in reaching out to the community. Together you can issue a formal report plus a press release, introduce it on social media, and add it to your website. You can deliver the report to your stakeholders and talk about it at events you attend. One of my favorites is to create a video like the one my Georgia Tech colleagues made called *The Georgia Tech Library: Engineered for You*. Animated by a local filmmaker and narrated by one of the librarians, it played a key role in our campaign to generate student support for the library renovation. (See figure 5.2 and a link to the YouTube video in the chapter note.)[1]

FIGURE 5.2
Still from *The Georgia Tech Library: Engineered for You*

You and your partners can serve as change agents by distributing the plan and asking for more feedback. You can invite people to visit the library or take them on tours, as we did. You and your partners can tell stories and ask members of the community to make the case by using their social media contacts. Remember that you are not asking permission to move forward with your plan. You are not looking for a savior who will take on your cause. You are not waiting to be noticed for the brilliance of your ideas. You believe in your plan and are committed to seeing it through. If you need resources, you will have work out how to ask for them or enlist others to ask with you. Your bold, public plan is your declaration to the community that you, your colleagues, and partners have listened and made good choices. You are a good investment. You are standing up for yourselves and for libraries.

Shift Your Approach

FROM	TO
Waiting for permission	Beginning work
Gathering more and more information	Acting on the information you have
Making a long list of problems	Deciding on your most important goal
Asking others to take responsibility for implementing your plan	Offering to share responsibility with partners
Keeping your plans quiet	Asking for feedback and distributing your plan widely

Activities

1. Explore ways for you and your colleagues to gather intelligence from your community and use what you learn to propose goals for action.
2. Share what you learn widely and ask for help in identifying partners.
3. Practice sharing responsibility for implementing your plan with your partners.
4. Apply a variety of strategies for making your plan public and visible to your community.
5. Evaluate how your plan is being received and if it needs to be refined.

Note

1. Georgia Tech Library, *The Georgia Tech Library: Engineered for You*, 2014, www.youtube.com/watch?v=8Rwj476Q2ek.

Action Step Four
Cultivate Relationships with Allies and Champions

> Your great mistake is to act the drama as if you are alone.
> —David Whyte, *Everything Is Waiting for You*

BY 2010, WE WERE ALL RECOVERING FROM THE WORST OF THE GREAT Recession. The Georgia Tech and Emory University libraries and the two university leadership teams began meeting in parallel about increasing collaboration between the two universities. Emory is a private research university whose main campus is six miles east of Georgia Tech's main campus, which is in the Midtown district in the center of Atlanta. Georgia Tech's president, G. P. Peterson, and Emory's president, James Wagner, were fellow engineers, colleagues, and long-term friends who were seeking mutually beneficial projects between their institutions. Their goal was to expand the formal relationship between Emory and Tech beyond the universities' shared biomedical engineering PhD program.

I proposed to Emory's university librarian that we begin exploring partnerships with Emory to improve access to collections and services for the faculty and students on both campuses. We hosted presentations and discussions about goals, projects, and priorities. Most of all, we wanted to create relationships among librarians as the first step toward cultivating allies and champions outside the library.

After many meetings, we finally identified our most important shared priority. At Georgia Tech we were actively seeking storage solutions for our print collections, and Emory University was beginning to do the same. Before

I arrived at Georgia Tech in 2008, the library had moved the university records and library journal volumes from a poorly maintained rental facility off campus to a warehouse in a light-industrial area about three miles to the northwest. Although this building was an improvement over the old one, it was not large enough or environmentally sound enough to safely house the majority of the library's physical collections, which we had promised to move in our "Georgia Tech Library 2020" report. For their part, Emory's library leadership wanted to free up space in Woodruff Library on campus in order to support their digital scholarship initiatives, house their growing special collections, and serve an expanding student body. Their library annex on the edge of campus was full, and Atlanta's High Museum of Art was anxious for Emory to vacate its rental space.

Things became more difficult in mid-2012 when Emory's university librarian and its provost both announced they were leaving for other positions. Because we were anxious to advance our collaboration without losing momentum, I redoubled my efforts to find new allies and champions among the leadership of both schools. I knew Georgia Tech's provost was on board with the collaboration, but we would have to start over in building relationships among Emory's senior leadership.

Knowing Emory's goals as well as Tech's, I argued that we should spend our time and energy creating a shared collection and storage facility in order to cost-effectively free up valuable central space for students and faculty on both campuses. Creating a shared collection made perfect sense because Georgia Tech and Emory University do not compete for students or faculty. Emory is a private university, while Georgia Tech is part of the publicly funded University System of Georgia. Thus, there is little direct competition between them for funding at the state or federal levels. Moreover, the local private foundations, many created by the families that invested in the early days of Coca-Cola, generally try to balance their donations between the two institutions.

Emory University primarily focuses on humanities and social sciences at the undergraduate level, while Georgia Tech specializes in science, computing, and engineering. Both Emory and Georgia Tech offer graduate degrees in business, but Emory has a law school, a theology school, and a medical school. Most of Georgia Tech's graduate degrees are earned in science, engineering, computer science, and architecture/design. The competition between the two schools' libraries is also minimal. Emory has strong philanthropic support for its library, while Georgia Tech has very little. Emory's library budget and collection are larger than Tech's, but its student body is smaller. The collection overlap between them at the time was only 17 percent.

Creating a shared collection and storage facility was the right strategy to fulfill both Georgia Tech and Emory's ambitions, but I knew it would be difficult to achieve. Internal and external politics in universities are complicated, and promising programs are easily derailed when key players leave or priorities change. In my previous jobs at Cornell University, Oregon State University, and Colorado State University, I had worked on three shared storage facilities, one of which was actually built at Cornell in 1997. A lack of support from local university leadership killed the other two projects, however.

Getting approval for the Cornell project, which cost about $15 million in the mid-1990s, was a slow, complicated process. It took several years, numerous reports and studies, and endless meetings. In the early 1990s the Cornell Library had eighteen different units, with sixteen of them on the Ithaca campus, one in Geneva, New York, at the Agricultural Experiment Station, and one in New York City at the Medical College. Adding to the complexity, Cornell had multiple library budgets, reflecting its dual state and private funding and governance structure.

At the time, I was associate university librarian for public services for the whole Cornell library system in theory—but not in practice. I had far more responsibility than authority. I had the university's smaller libraries on both the private funding side and the state side reporting directly to me, including Fine Arts, Music, Management, Math, Physical Sciences, Engineering, Hotel, and Veterinary Medicine, Industrial and Labor Relations, and the Geneva Experiment Station. The last three libraries reported to college deans as well as to me. But in reality there was a constant effort, which was sometimes more of a struggle, to work out plans and strategies across budget and reporting lines. I described my job as talking people into things in the morning, out of things in the afternoon, and then repeating the process day after day. It was exhausting.

My years of persuading people were less useful for finding allies and champions than the fact that I was well-known on campus. I had social credit as a reliable, optimistic campus citizen and an energetic champion of making the library and Cornell better. I had a long history of participating in campus initiatives, from the cofounding of the Cornell Infant Care Center, to serving as a lifelong member of the Status of Women Committee. I was known as a passionate but polite disrupter by the central administration, and a stalwart partner on major technology projects. The relationships with campus service providers, especially with Cornell's Office of Information Technology, that I had developed over several years proved to be crucial in getting support for a new high-density storage facility.

I had previously secured the funding to install online circulation, and had managed three large-scale projects over three summers to apply 6,000,000 barcodes to books and other library materials. My goal was to tie the library together as one organization and simultaneously prevent the library's growing physical collections from taking over spaces and overwhelming staff support for services. At the time, the cataloging backlog was more than 170,000 volumes, and the smaller libraries were closing public spaces and filling them with books.

The Cornell Library already had a storage facility, the Library Annex, which was located on the east end of campus near the apple orchards, across the road from the College of Veterinary Medicine. It was a metal box building, with open-grid shelving holding up the roof. There was a small processing area, office space, and a preservation lab. Many of the books and journal volumes housed there were unprocessed gifts and older collections that lacked records, digital or paper.

As I pressed forward with finding allies and champions from outside the library to support building a large, preservation-quality storage facility to house rarely used collections, I was repeatedly asked two annoying questions. "Why do we need library buildings if scholarship is going digital, and why are we keeping these old books anyway if they are rarely or never used?" Then as now, the question behind the question is: "What good is a library that does not loan books?"

I tried all kinds of arguments. I talked about preserving older paper volumes that would not be converted to digital format soon, if ever. I demonstrated that librarians and library staff are educators who help people find and use materials and not mere book handlers, as one irate faculty member called us. I jabbered on and on about using on-campus spaces for people and taking care of books in purpose-built, cold, dry facilities.

My colleagues and I developed numerous collection growth models, wrote page after page of explanations about the difference between a research

Action Step Four: Cultivate Relationships with Allies and Champions / 53

library and other academic libraries, and predicted that in the future libraries would steward historic paper collections and at the same time switch rising percentages of current acquisitions, especially journals, to digital formats. I went anywhere the audience would have me to plead my case for favoring people space over book space. In the middle of the political battle, I discovered that Harvard University had built the Harvard Depository, a cost-effective remote facility to free up campus space in crowded and expensive Cambridge, Massachusetts.

I set out to convince the university leadership that the only feasible way to grow the collections for research and teaching and at the same time preserve the on-campus space for students and faculty was to build a Harvard-style remote facility. The preservation argument appealed to faculty and librarians. The cost-effective argument appealed to campus administrators who were looking for ways to solve the current space crunch until acquiring paper formats would give way to purchasing digital collections. They were determined to avoid building more libraries in the future.

The two other library consortium projects for shared storage had failed due to inter-university politics. In 1999, when I arrived at Oregon State University, it had a mold-prone storage facility off campus that needed to be replaced. Under the auspices of the Orbis Cascade consortium, colleagues from the University of Oregon, Reed College, and I secured a small Mellon Foundation planning grant for a shared storage building. We toured warehouse facilities, visited the new ReCap facilities at Princeton University, and took our case to our respective institutions and our colleagues in the Orbis Cascade consortium.

We simply could not convince the university leadership or the librarians that an investment in shared storage would benefit all the campuses. They did not see that freeing up space for people on central campuses and at the same time providing high-quality space for the long-term stewardship of collections was worth the price. Some library directors saw storage as a threat to getting funding for renovations and additions. The conversations went round and round, with the same two questions that had dogged us at Cornell being asked over and over. In the end, our campaign never ended in a decision one way or another. We and our planning report were ignored. We failed to find and cultivate allies and champions both inside and outside the libraries, and our project died a slow death.

The same annoying questions about whether a library without books is still a library came up again when I was dean of libraries at Colorado State University (CSU). The University of Colorado and the University of Denver had built a Harvard-style, high-density storage facility, PASCAL, in 2001. But by 2004 their libraries needed still more space to store their physical collections. PASCAL was already full to capacity, and the library directors were looking for ways to finance the construction of a second module to house 2,000,000 items. After months of discussion and study, we came up with a plan to fund another module by a collaboration between CSU and the universities of Colorado and Denver.

I begged our university to invest in an expanded PASCAL because I wanted to move CSU's collections that had survived the 1997 flood out of a poorly maintained facility to one that would be environmentally sound and provide good service. My goal was to free up thousands of square feet on the central campus for people, instead of rarely used government documents and paper journals. Although the project offered a reasonably priced way to solve a space problem, the will to collaborate among the three universities was not strong enough to make the partnership a reality. The CSU leadership was not interested in investing in its library or creating stronger partnerships with the University of Colorado. The University of Denver eventually made other storage arrangements because of the timing of their major renovation. PASCAL now houses only University of Colorado library collections and has never been expanded.

Fresh from these frustrating experiences, I was under no illusion that creating a close partnership with Emory University would be easy. In the summer of 2012, Emory named the university's CIO as head of the library. He was excited about expanding the collaboration with Georgia Tech. Like the allies and champions in the successful Cornell project, he viewed shared storage as a practical way to solve a space problem, not as a threat to his career or his deeply held values. We agreed to push forward through a narrowly open window of opportunity.

The first major step was to get the support of Emory and Tech's vice-presidents who oversaw finance, facilities, design, and construction. Emory's CIO and the head of the library reported directly to their vice-president, and I had a collegial relationship with Georgia Tech's vice-president through our many conversations about the "Library 2020" report. We had bonded in our ambition to renovate the library not long after I arrived on campus. We happened to

Action Step Four: Cultivate Relationships with Allies and Champions / 55

meet on the sidewalk outside the library and ended up imaging how we would build a new glass bridge between the 1950s and 1960s buildings to reveal the city skyline. The new bridge would be a portal, not a barrier.

After a few meetings and phone calls, Emory's vice-president directed their design and construction organization to begin the formal planning process for a new storage facility. Two of my Georgia Tech colleagues from our capital planning group were part of the process to hire an architect/planner in fall 2012 and write a feasibility study for the project. I traveled to Emory for frequent meetings and spent months providing documents and advice to the planning committee, which included an outside architectural firm, plus Emory and Georgia Tech planners.

While the feasibility study got under way, I was looking for a way to solve the major threat that could easily unravel the project: creating a legal, productive relationship between a private university and a public one that is part of a large state university system. I contacted the head of the unit on campus that managed licenses and partnerships in concert with Georgia Tech's legal department, with which I had worked on library issues. After considering the problem, they suggested that the university repurpose a long-term legal relationship with Emory, a 501(c)(3) private foundation named EmTech, which had originally been created for research purposes. Two of our champions on the leadership team, the provost and the vice-president for administration and finance, supported this plan and took on the task of getting Emory's leadership on board.

The final feasibility report strongly recommended a purpose-built storage facility based on the Harvard Depository and the more recent ReCap facility located on the Princeton University campus, a facility which Princeton shares with the New York Public Library and Columbia University. With the price estimated at over $25 million for a two million-volume storage module, plus service and work spaces, the leadership on both campuses required us to do more due diligence by investigating possible rental facilities instead. Once again, I was part of a group of real estate officers and planners who toured available office buildings, warehouses, and commercial buildings, most of which were poorly maintained or unsuitable for other reasons. The most enjoyable and valuable part of this process was working with a former Cornell colleague who now headed Georgia Tech's real estate department.

Just after I arrived at Georgia Tech in 2008, I crossed paths with this colleague, who had retired from Cornell University and moved south. We had first worked together at Cornell in the mid-1980s, when I and two other determined women launched a campaign for a day-care center for babies from eight weeks to eighteen months old. The university's senior vice-president, who was raised by a single mother in New York City, became our champion, and assigned one of the university's real estate staff members to help us. Little did I know that this real estate staffer and I would end up twenty-five years later looking for potential library storage facilities in Atlanta. He proved to be our most persistent and dedicated ally on the Emory collaboration project.

His boss, the executive vice-president for administration and finance, also emerged as one of our strongest champions, along with Georgia Tech's university architect. At first, they supported the project as a means to the larger goal of renovating Georgia Tech's existing library buildings, but as the project developed, they jumped in to ensure that Georgia Tech was an active capital partner in the planning and construction of the new facility. They assigned a senior architect who was familiar with the University System of Georgia's rules and regulations. They traveled downtown to drum up support for the public-private partnership with the leaders of the university system. They monitored the legal and financial relationships and made sure that the project stayed on time and on budget. On the academic side, the provosts of both universities supported the creation of a shared collection for the use of all students and faculty at both institutions. For the library, the Library Service Center was a magic ingredient that enabled the larger transformation of the entire library. It was the collection stewardship solution which inspired us to reimagine the library.

For the next eighteen months, the design and construction organizations and the libraries on both campuses worked together to make the Library Service Center a reality. We and our Emory library colleagues had seats at the table during the selection of the architect and construction manager. I used Georgia Tech library funds to hire two consultants, former colleagues of mine on the Cornell storage project, who proved invaluable in sharing their expertise about everything from estimating the costs of moving collections to the current standards for environmental conditions, and everything in-between. The libraries scheduled meetings on one campus or another to support a network of teams that were writing policies and procedures. Legal support came from both campuses to navigate the complexities of creating a legal entity that

Action Step Four: Cultivate Relationships with Allies and Champions / 57

met the requirements of Emory's board of trustees and Georgia Tech's governing bodies. This was the most extensive collaboration I have ever been a part of in my career; it renewed my faith in individuals and organizations coming together for a common purpose.

The new Library Service Center (figure 6.1) opened in the summer of 2016. By then, the movement of collections to the new facility was complete. Emory was able to clear out its rental storage space and that on-campus location. The Library Service Center's new manager and staff worked alongside people from both libraries to address the remaining building issues and put new services in place. About 95 percent of the Georgia Tech Library's physical collections are now housed in the Library Service Center. Today, the libraries of both universities continue to build the shared collection to the extent that licensing agreements and different parent organizations allow. The management of the Library Service Center is in capable hands, and its operations are organized through legal and financial agreements that clearly define roles and responsibilities. I hope that in the future the two libraries will come together again to collaborate on new initiatives.[1]

FIGURE 6.1
Library Service Center

Takeaways

I am telling you these stories about Georgia Tech and other collaborations to encourage you to cultivate allies and champions. In making your bold plan, you probably developed partnerships. Some of those partners may be allies, but to make your plan a reality—especially if, like a building renovation, it requires significant financial resources—you must focus on finding influential people who have ties to funders and political supporters.

In making your plan, you have probably already built connections to people in your partner organizations and your community. Ask them to verify and add names to your list of the people whose support you need to move forward. To get the Emory and Georgia Tech library collaboration started, we had to be deliberate and imaginative about finding influential people who were willing to listen to our ideas. We got help from senior leadership, as well as from colleagues across the campuses and in the USG office.

I recommend that you think like a development officer who is looking for donor prospects. Keep preparing lists of leaders and influencers, and then find ways to contact them. Go to events and introduce yourself to people you don't know. Practice explaining how your interests align. Get out your well-honed information interviewing skills and set up some meetings. This time you are not asking how people work or solve problems, but about what interests them and their colleagues. Learn about the issues they are addressing that might dovetail with yours. Look for commonalities and possibilities.

I can almost hear you wondering if I am asking you to stalk people. No, I am not. I am asking you to sell your plan by finding allies and champions who will use their influence on your behalf. I admit that this process can be discouraging. People may not want to hear another word about libraries. They may not want to see your video or read your pitch. They may want you to go away, and at that point you should do just that. But the next day, get out your list and keep cultivating new prospects—and keep cultivating your relationships with those who are already helping you realize your library's dreams. And just like your mother told you, keep writing thank-you notes.

Here is a story that might give you some ideas. Imagine you are a librarian named Yusef. You and your colleagues in the college library have a bold, public plan to create a virtual digital art exhibit to showcase the work of students and faculty members. Your college is trying to get involved in the growing movie and television industry in town, and your library is committed to doing its part. You and your colleagues are willing to work hard on the technology and marketing required to pull off the project, but you need the support and encouragement of the art department faculty and technology services to select the artworks, judge the competition, and make it all available online. Some of the art faculty are aloof, and others are critical of the library's plans for digital collections. They like their paper.

You're sure that it's not going to work to just show up at an art department meeting to plead your case. So you decide to approach the problem of finding allies and champions indirectly. You remember that two of the early career faculty asked you to work with their students on digital art projects. You send them a short e-mail asking for a brief conversation with them about the project. You explain why you want to have the art show and ask for their help talking with the chair and others in the art department. You stop by your director's office to ask if she can help by contacting the provost, and whether she knows anyone who might be excited about the art exhibit project. The director promises to contact a TV producer and head of a small media company who is a neighborhood friend.

Meanwhile, one of your colleagues, Antonio, offers to talk to students about the art exhibit and find out if they are likely to submit their work. You, Antonio, and two other librarians go to the local art museum to see its collections and talk to the visitors there. You read about the movie and TV industry in town and find out why the college wants a closer relationship with them. When you ask your colleagues to identify people on campus who want closer ties to the media companies, you discover that Julie is an avid reader of local political and business news. She is eager to help by contacting movie and TV supporters for informational interviews.

Later, after carefully preparing a short video presentation about the digital art exhibit with quotes from the TV producer and the museum director about their enthusiasm for the project, you schedule a meeting with the head of the art department and the provost to make the case for the library taking the lead. You know what you and your colleagues are willing and able to do, and you are clear about the help and support you need. Prior to the in-person meeting, you post your plan on the library's website and social media to generate excitement. You are determined to find supporters for this plan, but most of all you want to forge lasting relationships with other people and organizations for events in the future. Because of your experience with getting to know the museum staff, you offer your time and energy to help with cartooning programs for kids on Saturdays.

This example illustrates that taking the time to know about your community will help you plan an effective strategy for achieving your library's goals. Find other people who support your idea and ask them to help you—and remember that no one of us is as smart as all of us working together. When you turn yourself outward, you are helping turn your colleagues and your library toward your community.

Shift Your Approach

FROM	TO
Exploring alone	Exploring with others
Waiting for allies and champions to appear	Seeking out allies and champions
Asking for support	Creating partnerships
Ignoring your environment	Paying close attention to political and social issues and changes
Assuming that allies from the past can be ignored	Nurturing relationships with current and potential allies and champions

Activities

1. Explore the political, decision-making environment in your organization and community.
2. Share the work of identifying and contacting allies and champions with your colleagues and partners.
3. Practice making contacts and communicating why supporting your plan is worthwhile.
4. Apply your informational interviewing and other skills to cultivate allies and champions.
5. Evaluate your progress by continuing to build your partnerships and keep champions and allies informed.

Note

1. Emory Libraries, https://libraries.emory.edu/maps/library-service-center.html; Georgia Tech Library, https://library.gatech.edu/lsc.

Action Step Five
Create Successful Change

> The Solarians have given up something mankind has had for a million years; something worth more than atomic power, cities, agriculture, tools, fire, everything; because it's something that made everything possible . . . The tribe, sir. Cooperation between individuals.
> —Isaac Asimov, *The Naked Sun*

AT GEORGIA TECH, WHILE WE WERE BUSY MANAGING ACCREDITATION for the campus, we also labored to build our leadership capacity, actively plan the prospective renovation of Crosland Tower, and maintain our library's existing operations. By the time Georgia Tech's accreditation review wound down late in 2015, we had to make up for lost time. Despite suffering from what we called "accreditation-induced post-traumatic stress," we had to apply ourselves to changing our library's organizational culture, leading and managing transitions, and working together as a team. We needed a framework for making decisions and staying on task in the short term and setting up ways we would interact with each other and our community going forward.

After discussing these challenges with one of our campus champions, the newly appointed leader of Georgia Tech Strategic Consulting (GTSC) volunteered their services to help us with leadership development and project management. It was perfect timing, and so I eagerly agreed. One of their consultants, who had experience in health care, manufacturing, and higher education, set to work to get us back on track as a leadership team that would be focused solely on the library, instead of being pulled in multiple directions.

I hated to admit that we were a fragmented organization filled with individuals who wanted to get on with their own agendas, often consulting others only when necessary. I knew that many managers were reluctant to make decisions and express their opinions about the needs of the entire library. Moving too fast in too many directions at the same time had created a siloed workplace in which we often focused only on our own immediate priorities. It would have been easy to blame our troubles on operating in six locations, four on campus and two at a distance. Although we were scattered because of the renovation of Crosland Tower, the real problem was that we were not a team working toward the same vision. Trust was low, gossip was rife, and the relationships among work groups were tenuous at best.

For the next eighteen months, we looked carefully at our decision-making, communications, and change management practices. With help from GTSC, we worked on defining levels of authority and responsibility as a means of becoming a more trusting leadership team. By June 2017 we had an updated statement on our mission, vision, values, goals, objectives, and tactics in which we declared that we wanted to clarify our purpose, envision our desired future, and define our path forward (see appendix A). I especially liked the mission, vision, and value statements.

While these conversations were going on, I worried that we would not be able to manage all this change simultaneously. I became obsessed with encouraging teamwork and learning how other successful organizations helped employees work together toward a common goal. Rather than remembering the long-ago advice from a previous boss about slowing down to let others catch up, I plowed on. Before long, I was living with the reality that organizational culture is a mighty force against change.

Like many other misguided leaders trying to bulldoze through major cultural changes, I went back to what I knew. Ever the optimist, I hoped I could manage my way out of our problems with such techniques as total quality management (TQM), supply chain planning, and Lean manufacturing concepts, which I had learned about in projects over the course of twenty years. My large technology projects and my first collection storage project back in the early 1990s had coincided with the brief period of interest in total quality management in libraries.

At Cornell University and nationally, I had championed streamlining processes such as interlibrary loan, binding, brief cataloging, and online circulation in order to improve services to students and faculty. Although my enthusiasm sometimes made me a menace who annoyed those around me,

I was thrilled at the opportunity to work on service improvements such as RAPIDILL, Ariel, brief cataloging, international and federal document collections reorganizing, preservation strategies, and online reference services.

What intrigued me about TQM was its emphasis on the same goals I had for public services. TQM was all about continuously improving customer outcomes while making operations more efficient, allowing the organization to direct more of its resources toward high-impact activities. Although some research libraries had implemented TQM in meaningful ways, mostly on a small scale, the Cornell Library was not one of them.

Total quality management is supposed to involve the entire organization and all of its employees in focusing on customers. It includes process redesign, integration, and continual improvement. TQM implementation also relies on fact-based decision-making, which was rare in libraries at the time, mostly because we did not have sufficient analytical tools. At Cornell we had experimented with process improvement and assessment, but we never attempted to include all employees. But the multiple sources of funding for the library, the independence of many departments, and the limited enthusiasm for adapting commercial practices and business jargon in a higher education setting made a system-wide approach impossible.

Because I was responsible for managing services across a complex, decentralized library organization, I was interested in breaking down barriers among the libraries on the Cornell campus. I chaired a public services council with representatives from all the libraries at Cornell, including the ones with different revenue streams from various colleges and the State University of New York units. After changing the library's name back to Cornell University Library from Cornell University Libraries, we implemented the first campus-wide online catalog; stopped charging daily overdue fines; and created campus-wide service policies, especially in circulation and interlibrary loan. We successfully made the case for high-density storage in order to free up space on campus for people rather than reserving it for rarely used library books and journals. We did basic surveys of students and faculty members' opinions about library services. We quietly used TQM's principles to move the library forward as a single organization focused on the needs of faculty and students. And because we made our changes slowly and quietly, we avoided generating a backlash from the more traditional people inside and outside the library.

When I arrived at Oregon State University in 1999, they were already benefiting from changes in technical services made under a TQM program initiated by the university. The university librarian told me that TQM was slowly creating a culture of customer service and quality improvement, and the library faculty and staff were becoming more skillful at using teams and TQM practices to solve problems. A few months later the university administration changed, and the merger between the library and computing dissolved. Complicated university policies and state-wide financial pressures ended all the continuous improvement programs, but the library faculty and staff were still using some of the practices during my time there.

At Georgia Tech, the library had initiated an extensive TQM-based action plan in 1990, though by its own admission the library lacked the statistical tools for evaluating the plan's progress. By the time I became dean in 2008, there was little evidence of formal TQM methods except for a strong focus on student needs and involvement, which was unusual at the time for a research university library. Students were regular participants in designing services and spaces as funding became available, a tradition that would serve us well in the subsequent renovation process.

Despite being aware of the fairly limited success of TQM in libraries and the strong cultural resistance to improvements based on business processes, I was so desperate to deal with our teamwork problems at Georgia Tech that I turned to supply-chain thinking and Lean process management from my various storage facility projects at Cornell, Oregon, and Colorado. With our partners in GTSC and a few key library managers, especially those who had previously worked in nonprofit organizations and commercial businesses, I decided to hire an industrial engineer to thoroughly map and review our library operations, including acquisitions, cataloging, reserve, and interlibrary loan.

This consultant, a Georgia Tech graduate in industrial and systems engineering, was well qualified to produce process diagrams after interviewing all the staff and library faculty involved. Their task was to group like processes together to determine their similarities and differences, and to diagram workflows. My goal was to create a single technical services operations team whose members were trained to switch from one operation to another as demand required. I was convinced that we needed to meet different high-demand times for interlibrary loan, reserves, and acquisitions as the academic year ebbed and flowed, and fill in the slower times with standard work such as cataloging and processing documents. Our consultant produced a book of process maps that were used to organize the work into a supply chain model—sourcing, fulfillment, and invoicing.

The consultant had difficulty mapping these activities, which had developed over decades and were broken into workflows by format such as CDs, digital content, monographs, and serials. The staff members could explain what they were doing, but sometimes they couldn't explain why they were doing it. Some middle management supervisors resisted the fact-finding process, making it difficult for the consultant to make steady progress. A few people in leadership positions stood on the sidelines, not criticizing, but not contributing either.

Through numerous conversations, meetings, reports, and explanations, I thought I was generating support internally. I wanted to break up the small departments, develop a new team structure, and develop new job descriptions that would reflect the library of tomorrow, not the library of thirty years ago. I was carried away by my plan to reduce the amount of time and money we were spending on processing and reprocessing paper materials so we could redirect our resources to front-line services. I knew I had at least tacit support from Georgia Tech's leadership for these reorganizing efforts, but I could not have been more wrong about having support from inside the library. I was so determined to move forward that I made the rookie mistake of taking silence for agreement.

Assuming I had support from inside the library, I also had to get approval from Georgia Tech Human Resources and the University System of Georgia. After multiple job description reviews, justifications, and modifications, the question of how to place employees into new jobs was still not resolved. We were trying to make radical changes while being fair to current employees, which is never an easy balance. In the end, we were told that the only reasonable way forward was to lay everyone off in the affected departments and invite them all to apply for the new positions. We posted the jobs internally in the university, coached employees through the process of writing their resumes and interviewing, and then hired them back into new jobs. A few employees chose to retire or leave, but most came back into dramatically different job descriptions in an almost flat organization. Three team leaders were competitively chosen from among current employees.

Despite the university renovating the rented off-site building housing the new organization, and the library funding many hours of training and skill-building, few people were happy with the outcome. Many employees disliked the new work space and organization. They wanted to stay in their old roles with their friends. They wanted to perform work they had been doing for years, not learn a dozen new processes required because of the fragmentation of library software applications. The managers struggled to sort out the workflows and the needs for additional training. Our human resources business partner, tired of trying to balance all the competing forces, eventually left the university and went back to industry.

As time went on, there were more minor and major conflicts among employees. Some of them were hushed up among the combatants, but others finally reached a pitch that required intervention. Although pressed to conduct another employee engagement survey, I steadfastly refused. The last time we did one was a disaster that still haunted us. All of these incidents kept me up at night, but I mistakenly thought they were merely symptoms of too much change, too fast. Once again, I was confusing hope with reality—these conflicts were actually evidence that the organizational culture was a mighty force chaining us to the past. And that culture was not going to change quietly or anytime soon.

Rather than initiating conversations in nonthreatening ways with employees throughout the library to find out what was really going on, the members of the leadership team and I chose a more formal process. With colleagues from GTSC, we tried to repair trust and promote teamwork with a variety of increasingly desperate activities. We talked with all the librarians and managers to create new job descriptions and update the USG job descriptions for all the staff. We reviewed once again the mission and vision statements and the action agenda, mostly as a way of building cohesion in the management group. We hired an outside consultant to take us through Patrick Lencioni's model in the book *The Five Behaviors of a Cohesive Team*. The leadership team and three other groups of librarians and managers did personality assessments and worked our way through the model's six lessons over the course of several months. We watched the videos and performed the exercises about the five dysfunctions—absence of trust, fear of conflict, lack of commitment, avoidance of team accountability, and inattention to team objectives.[1]

Our efforts were too little too late. The prevailing organizational culture was too strong to change, even slowly. The leadership team and I failed to deal with the sense of loss people in the organization felt. Our intentions were not malicious, but they were perceived that way by many employees and managers alike. I had deluded myself into thinking that I had the support of the leaders to make the organizational changes, but it was mostly acquiescence, not support. All those training sessions, reports, and discussions lulled me into a false sense that we were reimagining the library organization, as well as the renovated buildings and services. In reality, we were desperately going through the motions, hoping that something we did would fix our problems.

In the end we did make some successful organizational changes, especially in creating project teams to manage services, but more radical restructuring failed. The basic organization of the library remains similar to what it was when I arrived in 2008. Perhaps the effort might have been more successful if I and my colleagues had gone more slowly, making fewer changes at once. Perhaps we should have stopped more frequently to make sure people understood what we were trying to do. Perhaps we should have spent more time listening, and less time forging ahead. In the end, I learned personally and painfully why most organizational change fails; an organization's culture is indeed a powerful force pulling people back toward a comfortable, familiar past.

Takeaways

Unlike other stories in this book, this one is a cautionary tale. I have spent hundreds of hours going over and over in my mind what I could have done differently that would have produced a better outcome. On the positive side, I had plenty of passion, conviction, vision, and energy. I had help from many highly qualified individuals at Georgia Tech and elsewhere. I had courage, deep experience in libraries, and wide connections in the profession. On the negative side, I often misinterpreted silent acquiescence for support. I went too fast, relying on others to implement ideas without checking to make sure they were willing and able to do so. I thought that people were adjusting to change reasonably well, which for many was not the case. I didn't manage the narrative to ensure that people understood where we were going and the transition plan to get there.

Although organizational culture often mauls or destroys strategy, your story does not have to end this way. Before I give you some advice on how to avoid the mistakes I made, I want to reassure you that your efforts to change the culture of your organization in large or small ways don't have to have a negative outcome. You are not doomed to fail if you have a bold vision. You just need to temper your sense of urgency with prudent caution. Most important of all, make sure your strategy is supported by a foundation of honest cooperation and conversation.

My best advice is to take the time to deeply understand your organization's culture, its strengths and weaknesses, its individuals and groups, before you try to change it. I don't want you to abandon your principles or your dreams, but to appreciate how resistant organizational cultures are to change and how much individuals need help navigating from today into a new future. Make sure you take the time to acknowledge where you have been by honoring the past as well as creating a vision for the future. For small changes and big ones, you must provide a scaffold to help others understand how the transition will work from here to there.

Avoid employee engagement surveys like the plague. My experience is that at best they are not helpful, and at worst they are a disaster. If conducted at the wrong time, with the wrong instrument, or in a troubled organization, these surveys can make a bad situation worse. They bring out grievances and complaints which cannot be easily resolved, and they offer no guidance for strengthening the organization. It is far better for you and your colleagues to work in small groups discussing positive as well as negative issues, building your team's ability to manage conflict, and holding each other accountable for your shared vision.

Building trust, managing conflict, and strengthening accountability will take time and energy. Whether you are a manager or not, you and your colleagues must intentionally model these behaviors and practice them visibly day after day. You don't have to be formally organized into a self-governing team to create a close-knit group in which you trust each other to collaborate to get work done and extend your trusted relationships broadly throughout the organization.

For those of you who are managers, make sure that your colleagues and team members are not just going through the motions, and are afraid to admit that they don't support the plans being implemented. (For these employees, learning to speak truth to power is probably the most important skill to cultivate.) Try not to change too much too quickly, honor the past, help people feel competent, give people latitude to manage their own work and put some of that work on hold, and be honest about what you can and cannot control.

As William and Susan Bridges wrote in *Managing Transitions*: "Only people-like you—can recognize that change works only when it is accompanied by transition. Only people-like you can learn to manage transitions so the changes that trigger them aren't jeopardized. Only people-like you—can implement change in such a way that people actually get through it and the organization doesn't end up hurt rather than helped."[2]

Shift Your Approach

FROM	TO
Ignoring organizational culture	Learning your organizational culture
Focusing on your own agenda	Building teams with common goals
Announcing changes and then moving on	Building a vision and a scaffold to get there
Ignoring the past	Honoring past contributions
Choosing quick fixes like employee engagement surveys and personality profiles	Holding small group discussions about creating a shared culture

Activities

1. Explore your organization's culture and history.
2. Share in honest conversations with your colleagues about what parts of the culture need to change for your organization to change and grow.
3. Practice building trust, managing conflict, making commitments, practicing accountability, supporting group goals, and speaking truth to power every day.
4. Apply major changes slowly and carefully while checking to make sure that you and your colleagues support one another.
5. Evaluate how well change is going by having frequent conversations about the transition from the present to the future.

Notes

1. Patrick Lencioni, *The Five Behaviors of a Cohesive Team* (New York: John Wiley and Sons, 2014).
2. William Bridges and Susan Bridges, *Managing Transitions: Making the Most of Change* (Boston: Da Capo Books, 2016), 10.

Action Step Six
Implement a Framework for Action and Innovation

This is the middle.
Things have had time to get complicated,
messy, really. Nothing is simple anymore . . .
This is the thick of things.
So much is crowded into the middle—
. . . too much to name, too much to think about.
—Billy Collins, *Sailing Alone Around the Room:
New and Selected Poems*

MY GEORGIA TECH COLLEAGUES AND I WERE WORKING ON DECI-sion-making and leadership development in order to build trust in the organization, but we couldn't wait any longer to decide how to manage a large number of projects related to the renovation of Crosland Tower and Price Gilbert. Our library was still dispersed in six locations in a six-mile triangle in the center of Atlanta, with a hybrid organizational structure of hierarchical small departments and newly created teams. We no longer had the luxury of waiting to make it through the transition from the old way of doing things to the new way, because architects, engineers, and designers were expecting clarity from us on service spaces and technology in the renovated buildings.

Knowing we needed to create a framework for action in the midst of addressing larger organizational issues, I thought back to when we had negotiated the shared collection and built the Library Service Center in partnership with Emory University. Emory has a formal campus service for project management, with excellent staff. When the design project for the Library Service Center was approved, Emory assigned a project manager, who was a master at their job. At first, we complained frequently and obnoxiously about the formality of all the charters, reports, and approvals, but by the time the $26 million building project closed early and under budget, we were firm believers in both our manager and the process. We later hired them to teach some of our employees the basics because they wanted to learn enough to decide about taking the formal certification courses in project management.

To ensure that services were established and ready when the renovated buildings reopened, we identified more than thirty renovation design projects that needed attention. Georgia Tech Strategic Consulting recommended that we create a formal project portfolio structure of programs, projects, and teams, as well as proceed with plans to train project managers and team members. We needed more than a loosely configured group of teams. We needed a framework for action that would be tied to the available people and funding.

I enthusiastically agreed to the library becoming one of the early adopters of portfolio management on campus. When we were designing our portfolio of projects, I asked one of our own managers to collaborate closely with GTSC. I soon realized that we needed a full-time portfolio manager with experience managing a large number of projects simultaneously, one who could also guide project managers and teams through all the steps in the portfolio management process, from charter creation through closing-out documentation. Because the library did not have the funding for this position, GTSC and our champion in the university leadership agreed to hire a portfolio manager and assign that person full-time to us. Remembering our Emory experience, we were looking for someone with no ties to the library's existing organizational structure and politics. We needed someone with a fresh perspective and deep portfolio management skills.

Portfolio management offered us a disciplined framework for effectively managing the many projects stemming from the renovations. Because we were faced with considerable resistance to moving from small siloed departments to teams, I knew that we were not going to miraculously solve the library's organizational culture problems fast enough to design, implement, and manage the library services in the renovated buildings. To carry out our ambitious change agenda, I decided that we had to create a parallel organizational framework, the portfolio, to manage the work. If we did not redirect people's time and energy to high-priority projects and closely tie our technology resources to our priorities, we would have a building renovation, but not a transformation of the entire library. The portfolio framework offered us the opportunity to build expertise in cross-functional teams that would focus on the top priorities for the whole library and also build capacity for the future.

After years of managing technology projects in libraries, I knew that the portfolio framework gave us the best chance of aligning our technology resources with our plans for library services. The traditional library organization, in which technology resources are fought over by various departments, had frustrated me for years as I tried to implement service improvements. Every library in which I have worked has had too few technology staff, large amounts of systems administration and maintenance, and little flexibility in assigning people to new projects in which their talents and expertise are needed. Our field has trouble competing with industry when it comes to hiring skilled technology staff and keeping them. Our hierarchical organizations of small, overly specialized departments headed by librarians are at odds with the way technologists are trained and work in other industries. Library managers often insult the expertise of their technology staff by buying software and then demanding that the staff drop their other commitments and install it. Technology staff members get annoyed and angry that no one asks them if the software or hardware purchased fits into both the parent organization's and library's support framework. Consequently, turnover among them is high. Projects start, stall, and are abandoned. Resentment grows, and not much changes for the better.

I was excited that we were on a path forward as our new portfolio manager created a process to gather all of our projects into a formal structure. We began to understand the discipline required to operate in the portfolio framework. We could not afford commercial portfolio management software, so we used a variety of available tools, which were sometimes cumbersome, but with the portfolio manager's direction, we got started. We learned how to write charters, select employees for teams, prioritize projects, manage reports, and deal with problems and setbacks. We became accustomed to the vocabulary of subject matter experts: KPIs, Kaizen, level-set, and more. Our portfolio manager was teaching us the cadence of the project process with self-managing teams.

In the portfolio's first few months, projects were created for all of the services planned for the renovated buildings and online. As we became familiar with the process, we added projects that were not connected to the renovation, including white papers on topics such as the future of archives and the plans for the digital repository. At its largest, the portfolio contained 61 projects in 9 program areas. Many were small pieces of larger efforts, and half were focused on the renovation of the building. At any given time ten or more projects were on hold until we could return to them when people and resources were available.

Each of the project teams had library subject matter experts and technology staff who reviewed their plans and weighed in on implementation and support. We were modeling teamwork among groups who had only limited positive experience working together. At the same time, we were increasing our bench strength by insisting that the teams include people who wanted to contribute and were willing to learn, but who did not qualify as experts. Several library employees were funded to earn their certification in project management. There were formal training sessions in the specifics of Agile, Lean, and Scrum techniques for those who were interested.

Our employees worked hard, but they often struggled to keep up with their regular work while fulfilling as many as three team assignments each, plus consulting as subject matter experts on other teams. The library's leadership team gradually developed confidence setting priorities and allocating resources. The learning curve for some employees was steep, but most managed admirably. The final presentations were my favorite part of the process. I listened with pride and awe at the quality and thoughtfulness of the teams and their commitment to improving the library. The portfolio manager and I kept our champions in the loop by regularly reporting to members of Georgia Tech's executive leadership team.

But after eighteen months, complaints about the portfolio process, especially the large numbers of meetings and reports, were too loud to ignore. Employees were weary from working in two almost parallel organizations. Although we were making progress connecting technology resources to plans, people struggled with juggling their unit responsibilities and their project responsibilities. Some were enlivened by the challenge of working on new ideas with new people, while others merely tolerated it. We were definitely in what writers call the "muddy middle."

When the portfolio manager was pulled back into GTSC to work with other units on campus, we hired our own portfolio manager. Although there were problems, the first phase of portfolio management had succeeded in establishing a disciplined framework and managing all the work of the renovation and service improvement projects. Although I fully supported the continuation of

Action Step Six: Implement a Framework for Action and Innovation / 77

the portfolio, I was chagrined by dissension in the leadership team about the qualities and skills needed to keep the portfolio process going. I was surprised to hear that some people still insisted that the traditional library structure was effective in managing tens of projects across functional lines. I understood the desire for simpler, less time-consuming workflows and focusing on only the most pressing projects to get the renovation work done, but I didn't understand why we were still failing to connect our technology staff and resources with services. I firmly believed that the portfolio process gave us the best chance of making that a reality.

Facing the problems head-on was the only course of action I could see. I was determined to keep portfolio management, but first we needed to understand what the real issues were that were causing trouble. After lively debates and interviewing many candidates, we eventually hired a new portfolio manager from the tech industry who had years of project management experience. One of the members of the leadership team worked closely with the new manager to streamline the processes and documentation. GTSC led us through sometimes contentious meetings to sort out implementation issues and deal with issues of teamwork and decision-making.

The sole librarian in the library's information technology (IT) department became a key contributor to making the portfolio effective. Their efforts helped build stronger trust relationships between the technology and library employees. Serving as a translator and peacemaker, they gathered the library service employees and the IT employees into productive conversations about matching project goals and resources. In the course of explaining the purpose and value of portfolio management, they presented in a variety of formats, such as the poster for the 2019 Charleston Conference.[1] (See figure 8.1.)

Meanwhile, I decided to go on another campaign to convince my boss that we needed more skilled technology staff to transform the library. We had enough funding to hire our own portfolio manager from salary savings, but we didn't have enough skilled technologists to finish all the projects. I eventually secured funds for two new technology positions with salaries high enough that we could compete with commercial organizations in a tight labor market.

A new head of the IT department with experience in the technology industry was hired to work closely with the portfolio manager, as well as employees throughout the organization. With time and support, the library's IT department, portfolio manager, program leaders, and project managers sorted out

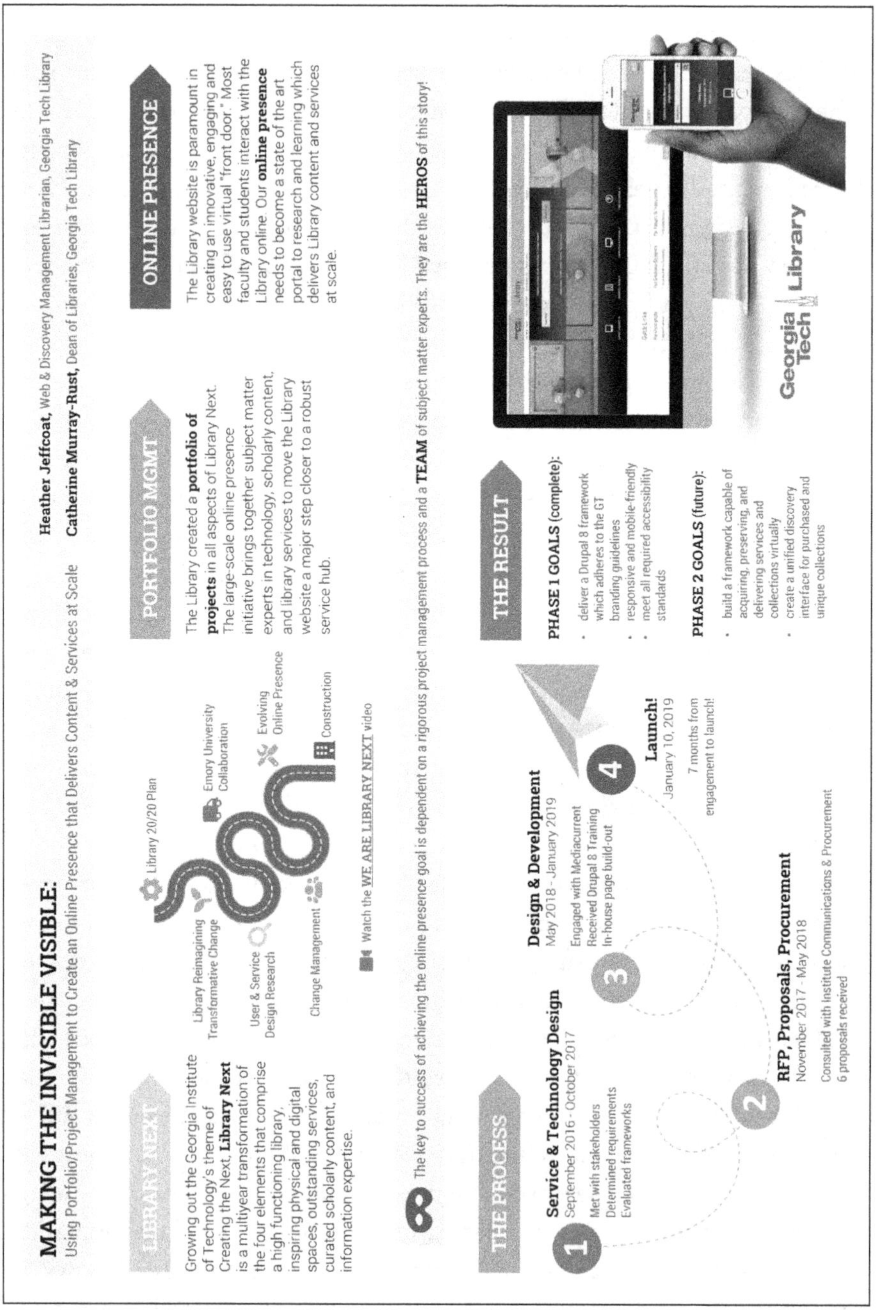

78 / Chapter 8

FIGURE 8.1
"Making the Invisible Visible"
Source: Heather Jeffcoat, Georgia Tech Library

the timely implementation of services in the renovated Crosland Tower. A key change was appointing a librarian or manager as the service owner for every service category planned for the renovated building and online. This librarian-manager and the IT professionals now work in sync on projects.

Thanks to key project leaders and team members' efforts, our linking of technology resources with library services was a success. The reopenings of Crosland Tower (January 2019) and the Price Gilbert building (mid-2020) on time were largely due to the skillful management of the projects in the portfolio. As the Price Gilbert status report (see appendix B) illustrates, portfolio management more than met our goals of building teamwork and capacity at a time when libraries need close collaboration to achieve a digital future.

After Crosland Tower reopened in early 2019, the project portfolio was scaled back from a parallel organizational framework to a more modest version of its former self. Our project management and teamwork remain strong, but the transition to a team-based organization never happened. It remains to be seen whether the portfolio structure and its benefits of building high-functioning teams of subject matter experts, technologists, and curious learners will continue in the future.

Going forward, I strongly believe that the library needs to encourage innovation. With the help of consultants, GTSC, and allies and champions, we adopted portfolio management to organize our ambitious agenda in a way that our traditional ways of doing business could not. As the renovations progressed, I worried that we were handling immediate needs, but not thinking enough about the framework we would put in place for the future. The traditional library organization works better when not much is changing in libraries and the outside world. The portfolio structure works best for implementing specific short-term projects. Neither framework helps us decide what we should be doing with our limited resources to further the aspirations of the community. To make those decisions, we need an innovation culture that encourages creative approaches as well as problem solutions. That is every library's challenge for the future.

Takeaways

My purpose with this story is to encourage you and your colleagues to adopt new frameworks for action and innovation. Based on my experience, using traditional library structures to decide what new work to do and how to get it done is no longer a viable option. The traditional framework is too individually focused, too fragmented, and too risk-averse to be effective in today's libraries. We need new frameworks, of which portfolio management is one, to move forward.

I took the risk of being an early adopter of portfolio management because we had no time and no good ideas about how to get all our work done with too few people while at the same time keeping operations going. For us at Georgia Tech, the portfolio provided discipline in a parallel structure because the traditional organizational structure was no longer adequate. Because of the portfolio's defined goals, participants, reporting, and documentation, it served us as a framework for managing new initiatives, especially complex ones. It had the added benefits of encouraging teamwork, valuing subject-matter expertise, and increasing organizational capacity. The individuals on the project groups learned from each other as they shared responsibility for the whole library's agenda and supported its success. Building organizational capacity, in my view, is even more valuable in the long term than getting individual projects done on time and on budget.

I strongly advise you to carefully look at how your organization or your team gets work done. You may like the structure you have in place. You may be trying to change how you relate to your colleagues in another part of the organization, or encourage a team to tackle a specific project. You may have deep feelings, positive or negative, about the value of teams. You may be frustrated, like I was, about conflicts among groups in your library that are preventing you from turning toward the community. For all of these reasons, you should carefully reconsider whether the framework in which you operate is serving you well. If it is, it can always be improved. If it is not, you need to change it.

Explore your alternatives. You might become familiar with project management by doing something simple like learning how to write a project charter and reporting forms. When the library hosted the Designing Libraries Conference in 2019, I wrote a charter, performed the steps to have it approved, asked the team members to contribute, held regular reporting meetings, evaluated the project, and closed it out. This process helped me organize a rather complicated event that was on the fast track. You can easily find examples of project charters and report forms and try your hand at using them.

If the discipline and structure of project management appeal to you as a way of organizing your work, you might consider taking a project management course or even earning your project manager certification, like several of my colleagues. If you have responsibility for other people in your organization, you might use your organizational interviewing skills to engage people in rapidly changing industries and ask them how they decide what work to do and what framework they use to do it.

I also advise you to look at techniques that are designed to encourage innovation—Agile, Scrum, and all the rest. Some are reputed to be more effective than others, depending on the organizational setting, but they are all worth considering. I find many of them, especially the Agile sprints, thought-provoking and fun. Many of the tools are open-source and easily available. You should engage with your colleagues as you explore frameworks for action and innovation that can connect you with the community and inspire your creativity.

Shift Your Approach

FROM	TO
Relying on traditional library structures to get work done	Exploring new frameworks to get work done
Jumping into work without a framework	Creating a framework that fits with your goals
Working without planning and reporting	Developing a disciplined process for planning, implementing, and evaluating
Sticking with your current skills	Learning new skills for action and innovation
Failing to change your framework as new goals emerge	Continually monitoring your framework and making changes over time

Activities

1. Explore what is effective and not effective in the ways you get your work done.
2. Share effective work strategies and frameworks with your colleagues.

3. Practice techniques like project portfolio management, Agile, Scrum, Lean, and others that might help you.
4. Apply a new framework and document your goals and progress.
5. Evaluate how well your new framework is helping you and your colleagues get work done, and then change it as necessary.

Note

1. Heather Jeffcoat and Catherine Murray-Rust, "Making the Invisible Visible: Using Portfolio Management to Create an Online Presence That Delivers Content and Services at Scale," poster presentation, Charleston Conference, 2019.

Action Step Seven
Focus on Impact

> It's always easier to think that your intentions are just as important as the outcome, but this isn't true. The outcome is everything. The outcome is what you live with.
> —Frances de Pontes Peebles, *The Air You Breathe*

Early in my time at Georgia Tech, I chaired the search committee for the vice-president for diversity and inclusion position. The successful candidate's main message during the interview was simple: the true measure of success for all equity efforts is whether they improve the lived experience of individuals. He supported creating plans to show good intentions and for documenting progress, but he was adamant that positive individual impact is the key. We in the library profession are beginning to turn our attention seriously to measuring and reporting the impact libraries have on individuals and communities. We need to answer the question, "What good did we do?"

I started my campaign to evaluate and measure library services and collections many years ago. While at Cornell University, I was responsible for completing annual surveys of our library to submit to various national organizations and the Association of Research Libraries (ARL). It was a tedious job that focused entirely on inputs. My colleagues and I reported on the amount of funding we were given. We counted the number of volumes we added to the collection. We filled in the questions about the number of books cataloged and circulated. We added document delivery and interlibrary loan counts for both borrowing and lending. We counted the number of government documents, CDs, and other formats. We didn't worry over how little we knew about what people did with all the books we bought and the interlibrary loans we processed. In effect, we were just crossing our fingers and hoping that we were adding value to the community.

To get some useful feedback in those days, I conducted mini-surveys. I organized exit polls about how many people came into the various campus libraries, how many students and faculty had an active circulation record, where people sat and why, and what people did when they were in the building. We mostly used the information to make decisions about spaces. For example, we found that students used the library between classes, and they chose seats where they could see a clock. (This, of course, was in the old days before most people had cell phones and laptops.) Although the information we collected was better than "gee-whiz" statistics, it was still closer to "fun facts" than it was to useful data for decision-making.

As a member and chair of several Library Administration and Management Association task forces and committees, I continued with limited success to look for evaluation and assessment tools and techniques that libraries could easily adopt. The public libraries had begun experimenting in the 1980s with output measures to generate data for decision-making. Typically, however, in academic communities the librarians professed that they already knew their communities well enough to evaluate their service effectiveness. They relied on the input measures from the ARL and the Higher Education General Survey—the precursor to the Integrated Postsecondary Education Data System—to compare their libraries to peer institutions.

Many librarians argued that their time or energy was better spent serving the community than conducting surveys and collecting user feedback. They either chose or were forced to rely on complaints as a way of measuring users' satisfaction with library services. The equation was simple: complaints = problems to solve, no complaints = no problems. Time and again I was told that asking users how the library was performing just annoyed people and encouraged them to ask for service improvements we could not deliver. Soliciting feedback would only make the situation worse.

I was discouraged, but I was not giving up. At Oregon State and Colorado State, I made little headway advocating for service assessment and quality reporting. People were overworked, and asking them to spending time on user engagement surveys was not reasonable. I figured that if I could find better survey instruments and evaluation techniques, I could persuade my colleagues that we could make more impactful decisions for the present and the future.

I explored the assessment programs at other research universities. I read all the ARL reports about data dashboards and attended some of their assessment conferences. The University of Washington's survey researcher accepted my invitation to come to Colorado State to advise and encourage us. I was intrigued by the University of Virginia's work on the balance scorecard and had several conversations with them. Although some of the tools were helpful in measuring the efficiency of business processes and gathering user opinions, none of them captured the story that I wanted to tell about the library's positive impact on the lived experience of individuals in our community.

In my early years at Georgia Tech, surviving the Great Recession without too much damage to our programs and services pushed assessment and evaluation right off the agenda. At the time the academic library community, inspired by the public libraries, began conducting return-on-investment studies to help their libraries recoup the funding lost during the bad budget years. In 2008 and 2010, universities tried to quantify their return on investment. Although some research academic libraries attempted to calculate their ROI, I didn't become involved because I knew these efforts would be ignored at Georgia Tech. Like the ARL statistics, the reports would not be enough to convince leadership to spend more money on the library.

When I became leader of Georgia Tech's ten-year reaffirmation of accreditation, I was thrown into the unfamiliar world of academic outcomes assessment. Creating specific outcome measures for academic programs to prove that students learned the concepts, techniques, and skills being taught was hard to put into practice. A few departments skillfully put measures in place. Others needed help writing their learning objectives and creating ways to measure student progress. We quickly learned that ensuring that the entire university adopted these assessment processes was unlikely to happen without years of effort.

The Georgia Tech Library sailed through its part of the accreditation report because of the measurement and evaluation we had done in the past, especially the playbook development for the library renovation plan which was running parallel to the accreditation process. Our user engagement librarian documented how the library assessed the value of its collections and services. They confirmed that we had active undergraduate, graduate, and faculty advisory committees with strong records of involvement in decision-making.

They reviewed all of our LibQUAL+ data from three rounds of the survey and summarized the well-organized input and output documentation which we had dutifully reported to national organizations. They made a strong and convincing case that the library uses all available tools and techniques to show the academic impact of its services and collections.

When the ten-year reaffirmation was complete and my responsibility for the accreditation process ended, I was discouraged at how little progress we were making in measuring the impact of our library services on the community. We still could not convincingly answer the question "What good did we do?" In my presentations about reimagining the library, I tried to persuade my audiences, largely unsuccessfully, that the library offers important contributions to the community—inspirational physical and digital spaces, information expertise, curated scholarly content, and outstanding services. I returned time and again to our mission and vision statements and our constant efforts to improve the value we add to user success. But I had no data or stories from individuals whose life and work had been improved due to our efforts.

We had dashboard data and other input measures, trouble tickets for technology issues, and user complaints. Our complaints were few, but they were serious and had usually been festering for a while. I especially disliked receiving angry and desperate e-mails from faculty and students who had reached the limits of their patience with service problems. All of these problems could have been addressed in a timely manner if the library regularly solicited feedback. Even a simple "how did we do?" request after service interactions such as book deliveries from storage and interlibrary loan would have been valuable. With feedback, we could have improved our services and better protected our reputation.

We still have not made progress soliciting customer reactions at the point of service, despite all my requests and suggestions. The reasons for this are both cultural and practical. Asking for feedback is too "commercial" and too difficult to collect with current tools. Time and attention have been scarce because of the renovation. Over the past few years, however, the library has made progress on other outcomes measures. It achieved a major upgrade of its website and its social media communications. Not only is the first part of website redesign complete, but the next major step is also planned. That one will turn the website from the secondary to the primary means of delivering services at scale. This transformation is scheduled after the renovation, when people turn their attention from the library's physical presence to its online presence.

During the years of advocating for the redesign of the library, my colleagues and I created several different tools to help us show our institution's impact. *The Georgia Tech Library: Engineered for You* is an animated video that we used to generate student support. Some of the librarians wrote a well-publicized white paper on why a library is still a library even if it doesn't have books. One librarian in the group gave a TED Talk on the same topic. WRECK radio, Georgia Tech's student-run radio station, broadcasts the only library rock and roll radio program in the world, hosted by some of the same librarians. Two years ago, the library's head of communications and I worked with a commercial firm to create a beautiful animated video, *We Are Library Next*, about the library's role in discovery and learning. (See figure 9.1, and the URL for the YouTube video in the chapter note.)[1]

Now that the renovation is complete and everyone has time to think about the future, I hope that my colleagues will use their creativity to implement new community engagement programs that generate stories from community members about what the library does for them. Such stories are invaluable in showing the library's positive impact on the lives of people in the community.

FIGURE 9.1
Still from the video *We Are Library Next*

Takeaways

I am telling you these stories to encourage you to focus on impact. Knowing what good you and your library are doing your community is the true measure of success. You may have discovered that there are many ways to evaluate and measure your work. Some of them are more effective in some organizations than in others. Some of them may be too expensive or too cumbersome for you to use. All of them take time to implement and demonstrate their usefulness. But in today's competitive world, you can no longer rely on input measures, respond only to complaints, and make decisions about services and collections based on your assumptions about the present and the future.

I am convinced that we need three different kinds of information to measure our impact. We need continuous feedback about service quality in order to improve current programs while protecting our reputation for excellence. We need ongoing conversations with community members about their aspirations, in order to guide our future choices about programs and services. And most of all, we need evidence of our impact on individuals—we need data to guide our decision-making, and we need stories that answer the question "What good did we do?"

Your library may already have programs in place to solicit feedback from users and nonusers about its services. If not, you might consider exploring Project Outcome, a toolkit developed by the Public Library Association (PLA), or Project Outcome for Academic Libraries, a toolkit based on the PLA kit, but which has been adapted by the ACRL for academic libraries. The Project Outcome toolkits help public and academic libraries measure and communicate the impact of their library programs and services. The free toolkits provide surveys and a powerful process for measuring and analyzing outcomes. They also include action strategies for using the results of those assessment tools. Since the PLA program, which was initially funded by the Gates Foundation, began in 2015, and the ACRL program started in 2019, more than 2,000 libraries have participated in Project Outcome and are creating a community of impact-conscious organizations.[2]

To initiate ongoing conversations with your community, I strongly recommend the Harwood Institute's Public Innovators Lab for Libraries. As I mentioned earlier in this book, the ALA and the Harwood Institute have worked together for several years to apply the Harwood programs to libraries. My colleagues and I had the opportunity to attend a three-day training session in 2019 which renewed my sense of urgency about turning myself and the library outward toward the community. The program workbook, along with Rich Harwood's books and frequent online presentations, are inspirational.[3]

Creating stories to illustrate impact is the next important step we in libraries need to take. A few libraries, such as the New York Public Library, have had fundraising campaigns featuring stories about their impact on individuals in New York. My suggestion for tackling this kind of impact reporting is to look carefully at how successful nonprofits present themselves. When I am asked to speak on strategic communications and the Georgia Tech experience, I usually talk about the charity that is closest to my heart, the Leukemia & Lymphoma Society (LLS).

The LLS began as one father's way of raising money for his daughter's cancer treatment by gathering a few of his friends together to run the New York City Marathon. Since then the LLS has grown and changed to keep up with the times. The LLS uses very simple and direct storytelling in print and video to show its impact on the lives of individual patients and families, as well as the participants in its programs such as Team in Training. For years, their stories about cancer research and treatments that went well and others that ended tragically have inspired me to action.[4]

Like the LLS, you can offer people in your community the opportunity to tell their stories about what your organization does for them. Today, we have a wide variety of tools and examples of effective storytelling to encourage people to join your team, be your ally, or become your champion. Stories help people feel at a visceral level that your organization makes a difference in ways that data can never do.

If your library has a fundraising organization such as a foundation, take the time to engage with the people there who are experts. They will give you information about what kind of impact information encourages people to support your library's activities. Successful fundraisers know that dramatic stories in which you and your library are the guide, not the hero, are the most effective ones. The fundraisers can tell you what stories motivate people in your specific community to act, and can put you in touch with audiovisual experts.

If you're going to invest your time and energy in one skill that will benefit your library in the coming years, learn to write and tell stories, and teach others to do the same. There are a number of inexpensive ways to become a storyteller. If you are a voracious reader, you have a head start. For me, and maybe for you, this part of measuring impact is much more fun than conducting surveys and putting up dashboards. Log into your favorite charity site and look at what they do. Evaluate your reactions to their presentations. Are you moved? Are you indifferent? Do you want to respond and ask for more information, or just walk away? This is all valuable information for knowing what makes a good story, so you can work with your users to enable them to tell theirs.

Here is a story that might give you some ideas. Imagine you are Yu Yan, a librarian who works in a university library. You have an idea about seeking support to teach students how to create persistent portfolios of their work. One of the university deans, a friend, suggests that the library would be an excellent place to offer online and in-person classes to students who are interested. You're worried about whether you have enough extra time to pilot this program, but you're sure it would benefit the students if they had a portfolio of their best work to show to prospective employers. You figure that if you can make the case for the program, you might get some funding from the colleges and the career center.

You set out to explore what other organizations are doing with online portfolios. You sit down with your dean friend and ask her what she wants to accomplish. You get in touch with students you have taught in the past and hold a focus group about how they might use a portfolio of their work. You share what you have learned with your colleague, Taylor, who races off to see if she can create a portfolio for her work. She promises to report back in a couple days.

When you are pretty sure this is a winning idea, you get two enthusiastic students together and offer to help them in return for their feedback. You tell them up-front that you want each of them to make a video explaining how they are going to use their portfolio, and giving the library credit for helping them. They agree, but they tell you they will need help making the video. "Of course," you reply. When you get back to your office, you hurriedly call your friend Sarah, who is responsible for the three-minute thesis competition on campus. You have been a judge for the competition, and you know that they teach graduate students to explain the impact of their research using only one slide and no notes. Sarah laughs and says that you are in luck. Training sessions for the next round begin the following week. You can't wait to get started.

Three weeks later, the students ask you to come watch their videos before they invite others from campus to see their work. They sit next to you in a darkened room. The undergraduate student, Lakshmi, appears on the screen with a huge portfolio case that is nearly as big as she is. She tries to open it and her drawings spill out all over the floor. She looks horrified and walks away. A few seconds later she comes back on-screen with a laptop. She slowly turns the computer, and the screen fills with a slide show of her artwork and her illustrated lab notes. Then she thanks you and the library for encouraging and guiding her project. Without your help, she says, she would not have been able to show her best work and keep it safe in a persistent portfolio. The video ends.

This example shows how to guide and encourage others to meet their goals and at the same time ask them to become advocates for you and your library. It is a reminder that the best impact stories are ones in which others are the heroes and the library is the trusted guide. You are turning yourself and your library outward when you are coaching others to achieve their dreams.

Shift Your Approach

FROM	TO
Relying on input measures	Learning about outcomes
Waiting for complaints to act	Continually soliciting feedback and acting on it
Talking only to your library colleagues	Engaging your community in conversations about your impact
Declaring your impact	Asking your community to verify your impact
Assuming the community know what good the library does	Telling your story and seeking user allies to tell how the library helps them achieve their goals

Activities

1. Explore how Project Outcome, the Public Innovators Lab for Libraries, and successful nonprofits focus on outcomes.
2. Share your best ideas with your colleagues and ask for theirs.

3. Practice techniques such as story-writing and storytelling to show your library's impact.
4. Apply your impact studies and stories to your library's community outreach.
5. Evaluate how well your library's impact message is reaching your community.

Notes

1. Charlie Bennett, "Reimagine Libraries," 2014, TED Talk, www.ted.com/tedx/events/10452; *Lost in the Stacks: The One and Only Research Library Rock and Roll Radio Show*, WRECK Radio, Atlanta, Georgia, www.lostinthestacks.org; Georgia Tech Library, *We Are Library Next*, animated film, available at www.youtube.com/watch?v=E-ARBadffpI.
2. Association of College and Research Libraries, "Project Outcome," https://acrl.projectoutcome.org/; American Library Association, Public Library Association, "Performance Measurement: Introduction to Project Outcome," www.ala.org/pla/initiatives/performancemeasurement.
3. Richard C. Harwood, *Stepping Forward: A Positive, Practical Path to Transform Our Communities and Our Lives* (Austin, TX: Greenleaf Book Group, 2019).
4. Leukemia & Lymphoma Society, www.lls.org.

Conclusion

Onward!

> I am calling on all of us to see ourselves as creators. We must recognize that we hold the power and the potential to shape the world we want. We are not powerless. We are not bereft of choices. Being passive is not an option.
> —Richard C. Harwood, *Stepping Forward: A Positive, Practical Path to Transform Our Communities and Our Lives*

Thank you for spending your precious time and energy with me and my colleagues through our stories in the pages of this book. As I wrote at the beginning, I am a self-described library disrupter, whose purpose is to help you and everyone who cares about libraries to create the future we want. We cannot stand by waiting patiently to be funded and appreciated for the work we do. We have to learn and grow to face the challenges ahead.

You came along as we traveled far and wide to learn about how other organizations operate. You, I hope, laughed a few times over our antics and our sometimes overly dramatic efforts to find supporters, allies, and champions for the library renovation and the Emory collaboration. You imagined yourself

Georgia Tech Library 2014 and 2020, north side
Photograph by David Hamilton

as Jenny, Yusef, Pat, and Yu Yan—my fictional librarians implementing new ideas. You read about our missteps and programs that didn't work out well, as well as our suggestions to help you do better than we did. I've tried not to brag too much about our stunning renovation of two old and crumbling buildings, but I'm sure you could tell that they are a dream come true for Georgia Tech—and for myself.

I promised at the outset that I would offer you seven action steps to help you navigate the future. All of these steps encourage you to explore, share, practice, adopt, and evaluate ideas and strategies. I proposed that you begin with yourself and expand outward to a wider circle of people and experiences. I asked you to be curious about the future and not get stuck in the present. I urged you to work with others to make bold, public plans that show your courage and commitment. I offered suggestions about how you can find and cultivate relationships with allies and champions and keep them engaged. I warned you about the mighty challenges of creating successful change, and I shared options to help you achieve better results. I suggested frameworks for action and innovation and urged you to focus on impact—to answer the most important question of all, "What good did we do?"

I hope that upon finishing this book you feel inspired to be a change agent. Think about the stories and the takeaways. Discuss the action steps with your colleagues and think of yourselves as teammates, not as individuals ignoring or competing with one another. Tell your own stories about what your work means to you and how you can make it better. Be generous with your knowledge and your time. Temper your courage with kindness. Laugh about your mistakes and be humble about your successes. Bigotry and injustice thrive on ignorance, whether intentional or not. Speak truth to power and stand up for the value of libraries. Through our work every day, we declare our belief that libraries can improve individual lives in communities everywhere. Turning your library outward is an act of defiance that the world needs right now. Onward!

Appendix A

Georgia Tech Library Revised Mission, Vision, Values, and Expected Behaviors

Georgia Tech Library Strategy: Mission, Vision, Values, Goals, Objectives and Tactics
Updated June 1, 2017

This document articulates the strategy for the Georgia Tech Library with a focus on the next 3 years. The purpose of this strategy is to:
- clarify our purpose
- envision our desired future
- define goals, objectives and strategies

Our Mission Statement defines the Library's purpose and our reason for existence. It will guide our actions and our guide decision-making.

Our Vision Statement stretches us toward an aspirational future and considers the anticipated future of the world around us.

OUR MISSION AND VISION

Mission: The GT Library exists to catalyze[1] the discovery and creation of knowledge.
[1] *NOTE: Merriam Webster defines a catalyst as an "agent that provokes or speeds significant change or action."*

Vision: GT Library redefines the technological research library of the 21st century. Students, faculty, and staff are inspired to create The Next through innovative digital and physical environments, curated scholarly content, outstanding services, and information expertise.

Our Values and Behaviors describe how we will carry out our mission and strive toward achieving our vision for the future. It is a set of guideposts for how we work together internally, and with the Georgia Tech community. These values and behaviors are the ways we will work to achieve our goals

OUR EXPECTED VALUES AND BEHAVIORS

1. **Integrity**: We promote collegiality, demonstrate ethical behavior, make data informed decisions, and strive to create an environment of trust.
2. **Excellence:** We pursue excellence by providing outstanding service and scholarly content and promoting innovation in support of research and learning.
3. **Impact:** We have impact on the Georgia Tech community by understanding and meeting customer needs, providing new learning resources, tools or solutions that result in new awareness or level of knowledge that did not previously exist, and soliciting and acting on valuable customer feedback to enhance outcomes.
4. **Curiosity:** We encourage intellectual curiosity and rigor in our organization and our services to faculty, students, and staff.
5. **Diversity & Inclusion:** We respect and support the inclusion of diverse ideas, cultures, perspectives, and experiences in the work we do.
6. **Communication**: We produce timely, accurate, consistent, and honest communication that promotes sharing of information and open discussion.

Goal #3- Internal/ Process: Library is adaptable to a changing environment

Objectives #1- Develop integrated workflow and process for the Library workforce that is customer focused by the end of 2017

   Tactic A. - Implement supply chain process for infrastructure and identify additional areas through the portfolio process and projects

Objective #2- The Library workforce is knowledgeable about integrated service- oriented workflows across the library by 2018

   Tactic A. - Implement Phase 1 in Infrastructure by end of 2017

   Tactic B. - Identify and Implement Phase 2 by end of 2018

   Tactic C. - Build skills that allow employees to work in more than one area in key areas (including but not limited to Infrastructure

   Tactic D. – Employees have an appreciation for the full lifecycle of the library workflow and the up and downstream impacts of their roles and responsibilities.

Objective #3- Engage in appreciating, investigating and recognizing changes around us through active listening and research by end of 2017

   Tactic A. -Implement the working Paper Series in 2017

   Tactic B. - Establish an annual review process and implementation of any opportunities

NOTE: This goal will require that people move beyond siloed thinking and knowing – that they understand what is happening across the library. These tactics will need to be embedded across the various projects and workplans

Goal #4- Financial: Library has sufficient financial resources to deliver service and content offerings

Objective # 1- Use data to drive decisions for Library operations budget for FY19 budget cycle

   Tactic A. – Hiring and operational investments are based on organizational needs

Objective #2- Develop a financial strategy that optimizes IT resources by FY19 budget cycle

Objective #3- Increase the investment in the library collections by demonstrating their impact on GT teaching, learning and research by the FY20 budget cycle

Georgia Tech Library Revised Mission, Vision, Values, and Expected Behaviors

Our Goals, Objectives, and Tactics are the approach we will take to fulfill our mission and achieve our aspirational vision for the future.

> **GOAL #1 COMMUNITY:** The Library is deeply engaged in the research, teaching and learning at Georgia
>
> **Objective # 1-** Develop a clear understanding of strategic stakeholders and their needs relative to the Library's vision and mission for each service area by Jan. 2018
>
> > **Tactic A.** - Identify list of strategic stakeholders for each service area (new and existing) in the Library portfolio by June 2017
> >
> > **Tactic B.** - Create a strategy to build the service initiatives with identified stakeholders by Dec. 2017
> >
> > **Tactic C.** - Leadership will prioritize the list of service initiatives based on strategic needs and available resources by Jan. 2018
>
> **Objective #2-** Actively engage faculty and students in establishing the service initiatives by Aug 2018
>
> **Objective #3 -** Establish a clear definition for identifying new and continuing user needs, and an ongoing process for the evaluation of current and proposed services to ensure alignment with the stakeholder requirements and the Library's goals, by Jan. 2019
>
> **GOAL # 2 WORKFORCE:** Library is an organization where high performing employees come, actively engage, grow and develop
>
> **Objective #1 -** Align organizational structure with the goals of the transformed library by the re-opening of Crosland Towers
>
> > **Tactic A.** - Produce a comprehensive reorganization plan for submission to OHR and the Provost by May 2017
>
> **Objective #2 -** Library staff and faculty understand their roles and responsibilities in the transformed library by the end of 2017 to have impact on the 2018 evaluation cycle
>
> > **Tactic A.** - Library Staff knows their roles and responsibilities in the transformed Library
> >
> > **Tactic B.** - Library Faculty knows their roles and responsibilities as GT instructional faculty
> >
> > **Tactic C.** - Broadly and clearly communicate so that Library staff and faculty roles and responsibilities and it is transparent to all in the organization
>
> **Objective #3 -** Library faculty and staff at all levels will seize opportunities develop new skills toward Library Next by the end of 2018
>
> > **Tactic A.** - Service delivery training program
> >
> > **Tactic B.** - Increase knowledge and skills in using computer applications (i.e. Microsoft products)
> >
> > **Tactic C.** - Create individual employee development plans

NOTE: As the Library develops new ways of working, it will be essential to have flexibility and agility for all roles. While we strive for clarity of everyone's roles, there will be fluidity in how people will contribute to the vision and goals of the Library.

Appendix A

Goal #5-Innovation: A redefined perception of the Library with outstanding virtual presence and physical spaces.

Objective #1- Georgia Tech Library pursues and implements opportunities in research, scholarship and services throughout the year

    Tactic A. - Library users find electronic resources needed for research and scholarship

Objective #2- Develop an virtual presence strategy by December 2017

    Tactic A. - Implementation of the existing online presence projects once approved

    Tactic B. - Develop a strategic plan and ongoing process for identification of new opportunities for online presence

Appendix B

Georgia Tech Library Portfolio Management
Example: Price Gilbert Computing Technology Project Status Report

Price Gilbert Computing Technology Status Report
6/16/2020 15:08

PROJECT NAME	Price Gilbert Computing Technology
PROJECT SPONSOR	Sam Graham
PROJECT MANAGER	Anita Lamb
PROGRAM MANAGER	Heather Jeffcoat
PROJECT COMPLETION	September 8, 2020

OVERALL PROJECT STATUS

- SUSPENDED
- ATTENTION NEEDED
- IN PROGRESS — Execution ON TRACK
- COMPLETE

NOTES: Change request approved for a new project schedule due to COVID-19. OIT CTS is in the process of installing software, deploying monitors and print kiosks. OIT AV is in the process of testing each zone. User training documentation is complete. Service Owner training will happen the last 2 weeks in July.

ZONE	READINESS	MILESTONES	NOTES
Library Store Service Owner: Karen Glover PG G240, G243		Validate Technology Requirements w/Service Owner Complete Computing Technology Design Service Owner Technology Design Sign-off Deploy & Test Existing Computing Technology Service Owner Testing & Sign-off	Library IT will support this zone. Printers and the new print kiosks have been installed. There will be 1 high-end black/white and 1 color printer in the Library Store. A total of 8 data ports in the floorbox still requested for the Bloomberg room (G243). Facilities provided 4 floorbox data ports & decided to utilize 4 wall ports to meet the need. The 2 expiring visitor PCs will be installed once data is available. See Service Readiness notes for more info & action log for updates. Meeting Notes Action Log
Research Consultation Service Owner: Cathy Carpenter PG G292, G266, G268		Validate Technology Requirements w/Service Owner Verify AV & Computing Technology Complete Computing Technology Design Service Owner Technology Design Sign-off Procure Computing Technology Deploy & Test Computing Technology Service Owner AV Testing & Sign-off Service Stakeholder Technology Training	Library IT & OIT AV will support this zone. Extron touch panels programming require resources to be onsite for any updates. This activity is still in progress. A PC will be in the private patent room (G292) and Library Facilities and Logistics will ensure a telephone line is in this room. Service Owner approved technology for the private Patent room (G292) and research consultation rooms (G266 & G268). See Service Readiness notes for more info & action log for updates. Meeting Notes Action Log
Scholars Event Network Service Owner: Catherine Manci PG 1280 Theater PG 2222 Public Programming PG 2202, 2204, 2216, 2217 Break Out Rooms PG 4222 Dissertation Defense		Validate Technology Requirements w/Service Owner Verify AV Technology Complete Computing Technology Design for Dissertation Defense Service Owner Technology Design Sign-off for Dissertation Defense Procure Computing Technology for Dissertation Defense Recording Deploy & Test Computing Technology Service Owner AV Testing & Sign-off Service Stakeholder Technology Training	OIT AV will support this zone. The AV design for the Dissertation room is a Day2 item. The SEN touch panel and streaming was tested successfully. The SEN touch panel programming and quality control is complete. The testing for the touch panel in the Break Out rooms are completed. The Technology Design & Installation for this space is managed by our Library Facilities & OIT AV teams. See Service Readiness notes for more info & action log for updates. Meeting Notes Action Log

Appendix B

Zone	Tasks	Notes
Media Scholarship Commons Service Owner: Alison Valk PG 3288 Video Recording Studio PG 3287 Audio Recording Studio PG 3286 Control Room PG 3210 Multimedia Zone PG 3204 Meeting Room PG 3201 Editing Room, PG 3222 Print Studio	Validate Technology Requirements w/Service Owner Verify AV Technology Complete Computing Technology Design Service Owner Technology Design Sign-off Procure Computing Technology Deploy & Test Computing Technology Service Owner AV Testing & Sign-off Service Stakeholder Technology Training	OIT AV & OIT CTS will support this zone. A proposal will be submitted for a green screen and curtains in the Video Recording Studio. A lighting engineer will be hired by OIT AV for the Video Recording Studio. Additional data ports requested in the Print Studio (3222). Due to a USG Apple contract dispute, the Mac PC order for the Editing Room and Multimedia zone was delayed until 02/19. Technology Installation is in process for the audio and video recording studio. Library IT presented the Technology Design to the Service Owners on 1/21/20. See meeting notes for more info & action log for updates. Meeting Notes Action Log
General Computing & Student Printing Service Owner: Bruce Henson PG 3230, PG 3250	Validate Technology Requirements w/Service Owner Verify Technology Complete Computing Technology Design Service Owner Technology Design Sign-off Procure Computing Technology Deploy & Test Computing Technology Service Owner Testing & Sign-off Service Stakeholder Technology Training	OIT CTS will support this zone. New color printers and touch screen print release kiosks were installed. Dual monitors have been installed. Dell PCs will have software installed. Service Owner approved the technology design and the seating change to 24 from 48 seats for 3230 & 3250. NOTE: The recent furniture floor plan shows the original layout.
Faculty Research Zone Service Owner: Liz Holdsworth PG 4230	Validate Technology Requirements w/Service Owner Verify No Technology Service Owner Sign-off	Service Owner approved there will be no technology in this zone. Service Readiness completed on 12/2/19, see meeting notes for more info & action log for updates. Meeting Notes Action Log
Instruction Service Owner: Alison Valk PG 4210 Teaching Studio, PG 4204 Capture Space PG 4212, 4214, 4215, 4216, 4217 Consultation CT 4160	Validate Technology Requirements w/Service Owner Verify AV Technology Complete Computing Technology Design Service Owner Technology Design Sign-off Procure Computing Technology Deploy & Test Computing Technology Service Owner AV Testing & Sign-off Service Stakeholder Technology Training	OIT AV will support this zone. Testing for the touch panel in the consultation rooms have been completed. The laptops for the Teaching Studio were repurposed in the midst of COVID-19. Library IT presented the technology design for the Teaching Studio (4210) and Capture Space (4203) to the Service Owner. Service Owner is aligned with the design. The consultation rooms were designed under the construction project and deployment is in process. PG 4212 is complete. Meeting Notes Action Log
Collaboration Rooms Service Owner: Bruce Henson PG/CT G116, G120, G192, G194, G201, G202	Validate Technology Requirements w/Service Owner Verify AV Technology Complete Computing Technology Design Procure Computing Technology Deploy & Test Computing Technology Service Owner AV Testing & Sign-off Service Stakeholder Technology Training	OIT AV will support this zone. The touch panels are fully functional in each room. Technology will be a Solstice and HDMI laptop connection in all the spaces except G120 (Willby Room). The Willby Room (G120) will have the same AV technology as the 2130 classroom. The Collaboration Rooms were designed under the construction project. The AV in the collaboration rooms are fully functional and the touch panel programming is complete.
Fire & Security Command Ctr Service Owner: Kim Mull	Validate Technology Requirements w/Service Owner Verify AV Technology Service Owner Technology Design Sign-off Deploy & Test Existing Computing Technology Service Owner Testing & Sign-off	Library IT supports this zone. The existing technology is working as intended and the Service Owner approved. Fire & Security Command Center moved into Price Gilbert on 02/17. Service Owner requested to move the existing technology on 02/14.

Source: Anita Lamb and Heather Jeffcoat, Georgia Tech Library

Index

A
academic outcomes assessment, 85–86
accountability, 70
accreditation review
    academic outcomes assessment for, 85–86
    of Georgia Tech Library, 17–18
ACRL (Association of College and Research Libraries), 88
action, 7
    See also framework for action/innovation
Action Step Five (Create Successful Change)
    activities for, 71
    approach, shifting, 71
    organizational culture change efforts at Georgia Tech, 66–69
    organizational culture, changing, 63–64
    overview of, 7
    takeaways about, 69–71
    TQM at Cornell University Library, 64–66
Action Step Four (Cultivate Relationships with Allies and Champions)
    activities for, 60
    approach, shifting, 60
    Cornell University Library's shared storage project, 51–54
    Georgia Tech Library/Emory University Libraries partnership, 49–51
    Library Service Center, design/construction of, 54–57
    overview of, 6–7
    takeaways about, 58–60
Action Step One (Look Outside Your Social Circle, Profession, and Organization for Ideas and Inspiration)
    activities for, 26
    approach, shifting, 26
    overview of, 6
    stories about, 17–23
    takeaways about, 23–26
Action Step Seven (Focus on Impact)
    activities for, 91–92
    approach, shifting, 91
    assessment of library's impact on individuals, 83–87
    overview of, 7–8
    takeaways about, 88–91
Action Step Six (Implement a Framework for Action and Innovation)
    activities for, 81–82
    approach, shifting, 81
    Georgia Tech Library's need for framework, 73–74
    "Making the Invisible Visible," 78
    overview of, 7
    portfolio management for, 74–76
    portfolio management, issues with, 76–77
    takeaways about, 79–81
    technology staff for library transformation, 77, 79
Action Step Three (Make Bold, Public Plans)
    activities for, 48
    approach, shifting, 48
    Clough Commons, opening of, 40–41
    Great Recession, impact on Georgia Tech Library, 39–40
    overview of, 6
    public plan for renovation of Georgia Tech Library, 41–45

102 / Index

Action Step Three (Make Bold, Public Plans) *(continued)*
   takeaways, 46–48
Action Step Two (Be Curious about the Future)
   activities for, 37
   approach, shifting, 36
   overview of, 6
   scenario planning story, 27–33
   takeaways, 33–36
action steps
   Action Step Five, 7
   Action Step Four, 6–7
   Action Step One, 6
   Action Step Seven, 7–8
   Action Step Six, 7
   Action Step Three, 6
   Action Step Two, 6
   conclusion about, 94
   introduction to, 5
activities
   for bold public plan, 48
   for curiosity about future, 37
   for focus on impact, 91–92
   for framework for action/innovation, 81–82
   for looking outside for ideas, 26
   for organizational culture change, 71
   for relationships with allies/champions, 60
   trying, 8
Agile, 76, 81
The Air You Breathe (Peebles), 83
   See also relationships
American Library Association (ALA), 32–33, 88–89
American Museum of Natural History, 20
appendices
   Georgia Tech Library Revised Mission, Vision, Values, and Expected Behaviors, 95–98
   Price Gilbert Computing Technology Project Status Report, 99–100
approach, shifting
   for bold public plan, 48
   for cultivation of allies/champions, 60
   for curiosity about future, 36
   for focus on impact, 91
   for framework for action/innovation, 81
   for looking outside for ideas, 26
   for organizational culture change, 71
architects
   for design of Library Service Center, 55, 56
   library renovation designs, 45
   for renovation of Georgia Tech Library buildings, 18
ARL
   See Association of Research Libraries
The ARL 2030 Scenarios: A User's Guide for Research Libraries, 28
Art as Therapy (Botton), 17
arts
   creative expression for learning about yourself, 15
   story about cultivation of allies/champions, 58–60
Asimov, Isaac, 63
assembly lines, 22–23
assessment
   focus on impact action step, 7–8
   impact of library, takeaways about focus on, 88–91
   of library's impact on individuals, 83–87
Association of College and Research Libraries (ACRL), 88
Association of Research Libraries (ARL)
   assessment reports, 85
   library assessment surveys for, 83, 84
   scenarios project, 27–33

B

barcodes project, 10, 52
behaviors
   of cohesive team, 68
   Georgia Tech Library Revised Mission, Vision, Values, and Expected Behaviors, 95–98
   modeling, 70
BNIM, ix
Bolles, Richard Nelson, 24
books
   barcodes project, 10
   Crosland Tower design for storage of, 42
   libraries, cause of, 4
   reading, 12
   renovation, public plan for, 44, 45, 46
   storage building for, 52–53
Boston's Museum of Science, 21
Botton, Alain de, 17
Bridges, William and Susan, 71
Brown, Brene, 15

C

career choice, 24–26
Carnegie, Andrew, 3
champions
   Cornell University Library's shared storage project, 51–54

Index / 103

cultivation of relationships with, 6-7
  of Georgia Tech Library, 93-94
  Georgia Tech Library/Emory University Libraries partnership, 49-51, 54-57
  takeaways about cultivation of, 58-60
  See also relationships
change
  Action Step Five (Create Successful Change), 63-71
  approach, shifting, 71
  community, turning library toward, 2-5
  COVID-19 pandemic's impact on libraries, vii-viii
  create successful change action step, 7
  library changes to meet community needs, 4
  organizational culture, changing, 63, 66-69
  takeaways about, 69-71
  TQM at Cornell University Library, 64-66
change agent, 94
charity
  philanthropy, engaging in, 14
  storytelling by charities, 89, 90
Clough Commons
  opening of/management of, 40-41
  pilot projects/user studies for, 18
coaching, 15
collaboration
  Cornell University Library's shared storage project, 51-54
  Georgia Tech Library/Emory University Libraries partnership, 49-51, 54-57
  takeaways about cultivation of allies/champions, 58-60
  See also partnerships
Collins, Billy, 73
Colorado State University (CSU)
  assessment of library services at, 84-85
  librarian lunchtime sessions at, 13
  shared storage project at, 54
communication, 12
community
  assessment of library's impact on individuals, 83-87
  bold public plan and, 46-48
  conversations, questions in, 32-33
  impact of library, takeaways about focus on, 88-91
  scenario planning exercise, 34-36
community, turning library toward
  as act of defiance, 94
  action steps, 6-8
  advice about, 8

change, urgency about, 2-3
  funding for libraries and, 3-4
  Georgia Tech Library's renovation, 1-2
  importance of, 4-5
  informational interviewing for, 25-26
  library aspirations rooted in community, 2
  value of libraries, 4
compact shelving, 18, 42
complaints
  about library service problems, 86
  for measurement of users' satisfaction, 84
conflict
  among employees, 68
  managing, 70
contact
  allies/champions, cultivation of, 58-60
  for informational interviewing, 24-25
conversations, 88-89
cooking program, 25
Cornell Infant Care Center, 51, 56
Cornell University Library
  assessment of library services at, 83-84
  barcode project at, 10
  shared storage project, 51-54
  TQM at, 64-65
courage
  asking for help, 15
  balance between kindness and, 10-11
  for curiosity about future, 36
  for informational interviewing, 24, 25
Couric, Katie, 10
COVID-19 pandemic, vii-viii
creative expression, 15
criticism, 10-11
Crosland Tower, Georgia Tech Library
  need for renovation of, 41-42
  planning for renovation of, 63
  project management needs for renovation, 73
  public plan for renovation of, 43-45
  renovation of, 64
  reopening of, 79
CSU
  See Colorado State University
culture, 79
  See also organizational culture
curiosity
  about future, 6, 33
  shifting approach for curiosity about future, 37
  See also Action Step Two (Be Curious about the Future)
customer service, 21-23

customers
    solicitation of customer feedback, 86
    TQM focus on, 65
    See also users

D

dance, 15
Dare to Lead (Brown), 15
decision-making
    assessment of library's impact and, 84–85, 88
    at Georgia Tech Library, 64
    scenario planning and, 30
    TQM and, 65
design process
    for library renovation, 45
    for Library Service Center, 56–57
Designing Libraries Conference, 19, 80
digital services
    of library, importance of, viii
    library building design for, 19–21
discipline, 36
Dorothy M. Crosland Tower
    See Crosland Tower, Georgia Tech Library
"the dripping water method," 44

E

Emory University Libraries
    collaboration, takeaways about, 58–60
    collaboration to build Library Service Center, 6–7
    Library Service Center for shared collection, 2
    partnership with Georgia Tech Library, 45, 49–51, 54–57
    project management for partnership to build LSC, 73–74
    thanks to colleagues at, ix
employee engagement surveys, 70
employees
    organizational culture, efforts to change, 63–69
    portfolio management and, 75–77
    takeaways about changing organizational culture, 69–71
    See also library staff
EmTech, 55
engagement, 24
evaluation
    See assessment
Everything Is Waiting for You (Whyte), 49

F

faculty
    future, curiosity about, 30–31, 32
    Georgia Tech Library renovation and, 44, 45
    library renovation project presentation to, 1
    Library Service Center for, 56
    shared collection and, 50, 53
    view of libraries, 3
fear
    of change, viii
    of future, 33
    of presenting, 13
feedback
    for assessment of library's impact, 84, 88
    from community for public plan, 46
    for self-awareness, 14
    solicitation of, 86
filters, 23–24
The Five Behaviors of a Cohesive Team (Lencioni), 68
The Five Things We Cannot Change: And the Happiness We Find by Embracing Them (Richo), 11
focus groups, 35–36
fortress, library as, 3, 32
framework for action/innovation
    activities for, 81–82
    approach, shifting, 81
    Georgia Tech Library's need for, 73–74
    implementation of, 7
    "Making the Invisible Visible," 78
    portfolio management for, 74–76
    portfolio management, issues with, 76–77
    takeaways about, 79–81
    technology staff for library transformation, 77, 79
funding
    for Cornell University Library's barcodes project, 52
    for Cornell University Library's shared storage project, 51
    historical/current funding for libraries, 3–4
fundraisers, 89
future
    active creation of, 93–94
    ARL scenarios project, 27–30
    curiosity about, 6
    exercise for scenario planning, 34–36
    future-facing conversations, 36
    scenario planning for library renovation, 30–33

shifting approach for curiosity about, 37
See also Action Step Two (Be Curious about the Future)

G
G. Wayne Clough Undergraduate Learning Commons
  See Clough Commons
Gaiman, Neil, 9
A Game of You (Gaiman), 9
Gates, Bill and Melinda, 3
Gates Foundation, 88
Georgia State University Library, 39
Georgia Tech Human Resources, 67
Georgia Tech Library
  accreditation review, 17-18
  action step stories about, 6-8
  after Great Recession, 39-40
  assessment of library's impact on individuals, 83, 85-87
  Catherine Murray-Rust's work at, viii, 9-10
  Clough Commons, opening of, 40-41
  collaboration, takeaways about, 58-60
  COVID-19 pandemic and, vii
  framework for action/innovation, 73-81
  partnership with Emory University Libraries, 49-51
  photos of, x, 93
  Price Gilbert Computing Technology Project Status Report, 99-100
  public plan for renovation of, 41-48
  renovation of, Action Step One stories, 18-21
  scenario planning project, 30-33
  stories about transformation of, 5, 93-94
  thanks to colleagues at, ix
  TQM methods at, 66
"Georgia Tech Library 2020" (Georgia Tech Library), 50
The Georgia Tech Library: Engineered for You (video), 47, 87
Georgia Tech Library Revised Mission, Vision, Values, and Expected Behaviors, 95-98
Georgia Tech Strategic Consulting (GTSC)
  help with transformation of library services, 7, 22
  leadership development/project management help from, 63-64
  library operations mapping/review, 66-69
  portfolio management and, 77
goals
  framework for action/innovation, 81-82

furthering other people's goals, 46
Georgia Tech Library renovation and, 31
Georgia Tech Library Revised Mission, Vision, Values, and Expected Behaviors, 97-98
knowledge of community and, 60
portfolio management and, 77, 79, 80
for shared collection, 50
teams with common goals, 71
of TQM, 65
Gorman, Michael, 4
Great Recession
  curiosity about future after, 27
  Georgia Tech Library's recovery from, 49
  Georgia Tech Library's survival during, 85
  impact on Georgia Tech Library, 10, 39-40
  renovation of library and, 44, 45
GTSC
  See Georgia Tech Strategic Consulting

H
Harvard Depository
  building of, 53
  storage facility design based on, 55
Harwood, Richard C., 89, 93
Harwood Institute Public Innovators Lab for Libraries, 32-33, 88-89
Heffernan, M. Paul, 42
High Museum of Art (Atlanta), 50
Higher Education General Survey, 84
Holzer, Jenny, 19

I
ideas
  See Action Step One (Look Outside Your Social Circle, Profession, and Organization for Ideas and Inspiration)
"imagine-you-are" story, 5
impact, focus on
  action step, 7-8
  activities for, 91-92
  approach, shifting, 91
  assessment of library's impact on individuals, 83-87
  takeaways about, 88-91
impact reporting, 7-8
individuals
  assessment of library's impact on individuals, 83-87
  impact of library, takeaways about focus on, 88-91
  See also users
informational interviewing, 24-26

innovation, 7, 81
  See also framework for action/innovation
inspiration, 6
  See also Action Step One (Look Outside
    Your Social Circle, Profession,
    and Organization for Ideas and
    Inspiration)
interactive media, 21
internet, viii
interviewing, informational, 24–26
introverts, 16, 24

J
Jeffcoat, Heather, 78
job descriptions, 67–68
journals, 39

K
kindness, 11
Klinenberg, Eric, 4

L
leadership
  action steps, viii
  development at Georgia Tech Library,
    63–64
  organizational culture, efforts to change,
    66–69
  portfolio management and, 76
  TQM and, 64–66
Lean process management, 64, 66, 76
learning
  about yourself, 11–12
  library design for, 19
legal support, 56–57
Lehman Brothers, 39
Lencioni, Patrick, 68
Leukemia & Lymphoma Society (LLS), 14, 89
librarians
  activities for learning about yourself, 12–16
  assessment of library's impact on
    individuals, 83–87
  change, dealing with, vii–viii
  future, active creation of, 93–94
  learning about yourself, 9–12
library
  assessment of library's impact on
    individuals, 83–87
  community, turning toward, 1–8
  COVID-19 pandemic's impact on, vii–viii
  future, active creation of, 93–94
  renovation, Action Step One stories about,
    18–21
  renovation, scenario planning and, 31–33

renovation, story about bold public plan
  for, 41–45
renovation, takeaways about bold public
  plan for, 46–48
renovation of Georgia Tech Library, 1–2
  value of, 4
"Library 2020" (Georgia Tech Library), 42–43
Library Annex, Cornell University Library, 52
library disruptor
  action steps for, viii
  role of, 93
library operations, 66–69
Library Service Center (LSC)
  collaboration to build, 6–7, 45
  construction of, 2
  Georgia Tech Library/Emory University
    Libraries partnership for, 49–51,
    54–57
  partnership steps for building of, 54–57
  photo of, 57
  project management for partnership to
    build, 73–74
library staff
  for management of Clough Commons,
    40–41
  organizational culture, efforts to change,
    63–69
  portfolio management and, 75–76
  portfolio manager, 74, 75
  takeaways about changing organizational
    culture, 69–71
  technology staff, 75, 77, 79
listening
  development of listening skills, 13
  in informational interviewing, 24
  turning library toward, 33
The Literature of Livelihood: Reading and
  Writing about Work" (Georgia Tech
  program), 24
LLS (Leukemia & Lymphoma Society), 14, 89
LSC
  See Library Service Center

M
"Making the Invisible Visible" (Georgia Tech
  Library poster), 78
*Managing Transitions: Making the Most of
  Change* (Bridges & Bridges), 71
manufacturing organizations, 22–23
mapping, of library operations, 66–69
Massachusetts Institute of Technology (MIT),
  21
Massachusetts Medical Center, 14
meditation, 14

meeting
- for community engagement projects, 35
- for cultivation of allies/champions, 58, 59-60
- for organizational change, 67

mental health, 9

mini-surveys, 84

mission statement
- Georgia Tech Library Revised Mission, Vision, Values, and Expected Behaviors, 64, 95-98
- library's impact on individuals and, 86
- review of, 68
- shared mission of libraries, 5

MIT (Massachusetts Institute of Technology), 21

Morgenstern, Erin, 27

Murray-Rust, Catherine
- Action Step Five story, 63-69
- Action Step Four stories, 49-57
- Action Step One stories, 17-23
- Action Step Seven story, 83-87
- Action Step Six story, 73-79
- Action Step Two stories, 27-33
- colon cancer diagnosis/treatments, 9-10
- Georgia Tech Library after economic recession, 39-40
- as library disruptor, 93
- public plan for renovation of Georgia Tech Library, 41-45

Museum of Science and Industry, 20

music, 15

N

The Naked Sun (Asimov), 63

National Diabetes Association, 25

National Gallery of Art, 19

New York Public Library, 89

The Night Circus (Morgenstern), 27

North Carolina State University, 19

O

Obama, Barack, 18

online portfolios, 90-91

online services, viii

operations
- Action Step One activities for improving, 21-23
- library operations mapping/review, 66-69

Orbis Cascade consortium, 53

Oregon State University
- assessment of library services at, 84-85
- shared storage project at, 53
- TQM at, 66

organizational capacity, 80

organizational culture
- efforts to change, 63-64
- operations mapping/review, 66-69
- portfolio management and, 74
- power to resist change, 7
- takeaways about changing, 69-71
- TQM at Cornell University Library, 64-65

Orlean, Susan
- *The Library Book*, vii
- on value of libraries, 4, 5

output measures, 84

P

Palaces for the People: How Social Infrastructure Can Help Fight Inequality, Polarization, and the Decline of Civic Life (Klinenberg), 4

partnerships
- bold public plan and, 46
- Cornell University Library's shared storage project, 51-54
- Georgia Tech Library/Emory University Libraries partnership, 49-51, 54-57
- project management for partnership to build LSC, 73-74
- for renovation of Georgia Tech Library, 45
- takeaways about cultivation of allies/champions, 58-60
- *See also* collaboration

PASCAL storage facility, 54

patrons
- *See* customers; users

Peebles, Frances de Pontes, 83

people, engaging with, 16

Peterson, G. P., 49

philanthropy, 14

pictures, in library plan, 47

Pixar exhibit, 21

PLA (Public Library Association), 88

planning
- exercise for scenario planning, 34-36
- scenario planning, 27-33

plans
- Action Step Three, 6
- bold public plan, story about, 41-45
- bold public plan, takeaways about, 46-48
- cultivation of allies/champions and, 58-59
- for Georgia Tech Library renovation, 39-41
- partnerships and, 58

platform, library as, 3

portfolio management
- for framework for action/innovation, 74-76

portfolio management *(continued)*
   issues with, 76-77
   "Making the Invisible Visible" poster, 78
   Price Gilbert Computing Technology Project Status Report, 99-100
   success of, 79
   takeaways about, 79-81
portfolio manager
   for Georgia Tech Library, 74
   hiring of, 76, 77
portfolios, student work, 90-91
Pratt, Enoch, 3
Praxis3, ix
presentation skills, 13
Price Gilbert Computing Technology Project Status Report, 99-100
Price Gilbert Memorial Library
   need for renovation of, 41-42
   project management needs for renovation, 73
   public plan for renovation of, 43-45
   reopening of, 79
problems
   complaints about library service problems, 86
   in exercise for scenario planning, 34-36
   user complaints and, 84
project management
   framework for action/innovation, need for, 73-74
   at Georgia Tech Library, 63-64
   portfolio management, 74-76
   portfolio management, issues with, 76-77
   takeaways about, 79-81
Project Outcome for Academic Libraries toolkit, 88
Project Outcome toolkit, 88
project portfolio management, 7
Public Innovators Lab for Libraries, Harwood Institute, Harwood Institute Public Innovators Lab for Libraries, 32-33, 88-89
Public Library Association (PLA), 88
public plan
   See plans
public speaking, 13

Q
questions
   for community conversations, 32
   cultivation of allies/champions and, 52, 53-54
   for engaging others, 24
   for informational interviewing, 25
   "What good did we do?," 94

R
radio station, 87
RAPID Interlibrary Loan, 39
reading, 12
relationships
   Cornell University Library's shared storage project, 51-54
   cultivation of with allies/champions, 6-7
   at Georgia Tech Library, 64
   Georgia Tech Library/Emory University Libraries partnership, 49-51, 54-57
   takeaways about cultivation of allies/champions, 58-60
   See also collaboration; partnerships
renovation
   Action Step One stories about, 18-21
   Crosland Tower/Price Gilbert Memorial Library, reopening of, 79
   of Georgia Tech Library, public plan for, 41-45
   of Georgia Tech Library, success of, 93-94
   Georgia Tech Library/Emory University Libraries partnership, 54-57
   portfolio management for, 74-76
   project management needs for, 73
   scenario planning and, 31-33
   takeaways about bold public plan for, 46-48
Renwick Gallery, 19-20
reports
   bold public plan, issuing, 47-48
   Georgia Tech's accreditation review, 17-18
   Price Gilbert Computing Technology Project Status Report, 99-100
   public plan for renovation of Georgia Tech Library, 42-45
research, 28-30
resources
   Georgia Tech Library Revised Mission, Vision, Values, and Expected Behaviors, 95-98
   Price Gilbert Computing Technology Project Status Report, 99-100
return-on-investment (ROI), 85
Richo, David, 11
Royal Dutch Shell, 27-28

S
Sailing Alone Around the Room: New and Selected Poems (Collins), 73

scenario planning
  critical uncertainties diagram, 29
  exercise for, 34–36
  techniques of, 27–33
scenarios project, 27–33
Scrum, 76, 81
security, 44, 45
self-awareness, 14
self-discovery, 11–12
Shambhala meditation program, 14
shared collection
  building of Library Service Center for, 45
  collaboration to build Library Service Center, 6–7
  Georgia Tech Library/Emory University Libraries partnership for, 49–51, 54–57
Shaw, George Bernard, 1
silence, 67, 69
social credit
  finding allies/champions and, 51–52
  for renovation of Georgia Tech Library, 41
  from work of library, 18
software, 75
Sontag, Susan, 39
spaces, 84
staff
  See employees; library staff
Stepping Forward: A Positive, Practical Path to Transform Our Communities and Our Lives (Harwood), 93
storage
  Colorado State University's shared storage project, 54
  Cornell University Library's shared storage project, 51–54
  Georgia Tech Library/Emory University Libraries partnership for creation of, 54–57
  Georgia Tech Library/Emory University Libraries partnership goal, 49–50, 51
stories
  about framework for action/innovation, 73–79
  about organizational culture change, 63–69
  Action Step One, 17–23
  Action Step Seven, 83–87
  Action Step Two, 27–33
  in action steps, 5–8
  benefit of listening to, 12
  from community members about library, 87
  Cornell University Library's shared storage project, 51–54
  Georgia Tech Library/Emory University Libraries partnership, 49–51, 54–57
  to illustrate library's impact, 89–90
  portfolios of student work, 90–91
  public plan for renovation of Georgia Tech Library, 41–45
students
  creative expression, 15
  Georgia Tech Library renovation and, 42, 44, 45
  informational interviewing and, 24
  Library Service Center for, 56
  portfolios of student work, 90–91
  shared collection and, 50, 53
  support for library renovation, 47
  TQM and, 66
  virtual digital art exhibit, 58–59
  visits to museums with, 21
success
  of Georgia Tech Library renovation, 93–94
  impact of library as measure of, 88
supply chain planning, 64, 66
support, 67, 69
surveys
  for assessment of library services, 83, 84–85
  employee engagement surveys, 70

T
takeaways
  about cultivation of allies/champions, 58–60
  about focus on impact, 88–91
  about learning about yourself, 11–12
  about organizational culture change, 69–71
  for Action Step One, 23–26
  for framework for action/innovation, 79–81
teams
  framework for action/innovation and, 80
  portfolio management and, 75–76
  project teams, creation of, 69
  teamwork, encouragement of, 64, 68
technology resources
  linking with library services, 79
  portfolio management for, 75
  project management for, 76
technology staff
  for library transformation, 77, 79
  portfolio management and, 76
TED Talk, 87
tests, 14

"This I Believe" piece, 12
total quality management (TQM)
 at Cornell University Library, 64–65
 at Georgia Tech Library, 66
 at Oregon State University, 66
tours
 of library buildings needing renovation, 44–45
 of storage facilities, 55
Toyota, 22–23
transitions, 71
travel
 for engaging with other people, 16
 for library building design ideas, 19–20
trust
 building, 70
 efforts to repair, 68

U
University of Calgary, 19
University of Denver, 54
University of Washington, 85
University System of Georgia (USG)
 capital construction projects on hold, 39
 Georgia Tech Library renovation and, 18
 public plan for renovation of Georgia Tech Library, 45
 support for organizational change, 67
university-based research, 28–30
users
 assessment of library's impact on individuals, 83–87
 impact of library, takeaways about focus on, 88–91
 solicitation of customer feedback, 86

V
values, 95–98

video
 for library renovation plan, 47
 student portfolio videos, 90–91
 We Are Library Next, 87
vision
 bold, 70
 for successful change, 71
vision statement
 Georgia Tech Library Revised Mission, Vision, Values, and Expected Behaviors, 64, 95–98
 library's impact on individuals and, 86
 review of, 68, 86

W
Wagner, James, 49
We Are Library Next (video), 87
website, 86–87
What Color Is Your Parachute? (Bolles), 24
"What good did we do?" question, 94
Whyte, David, 49
Woodruff Library, Emory University, 50
WRECK radio, 87
writing, 12

Y
yourself, beginning with
 coaching, 15
 creative expression, 15
 engaging with other people, 16
 listening, 13
 meditating, 14
 philanthropy, engaging in, 14
 presenting, 13
 reading for, 12
 self-awareness, 14
 stories about, 9–11
 takeaways, 11–12
 writing for, 12

CPSIA information can be obtained
at www.ICGtesting.com
Printed in the USA
JSHW020437051222
34273JS00003B/7